GERALD F. VAN ACKEREN, S. J.

SACRA DOCTRINA

THE SUBJECT OF THE FIRST QUESTION
OF THE *SUMMA THEOLOGICA* OF ST. THOMAS AQUINAS

WITH AN INTRODUCTION

BY

FR. YVES M. J. CONGAR, O.P.

ROMAE 1952

OFFICIUM LIBRI CATHOLICI - CATHOLIC BOOK AGENCY

IMPRIMATUR

E Vicariatu Urbis, die 15-VII-52

† ALOYSIUS TRAGLIA

Archiep.us Caesarien. Vicesgerens

Stabilimento tipografico S. Lapi - Città di Castello

DEDICATED DEVOTEDLY

TO

MY DAD

TABLE OF CONTENTS

PREFACE

The purpose of this study is to determine the subject that St. Thomas is investigating in the first question of his Summa Theologica. In other words, what does he mean by sacra doctrina, the term he uses to designate the subject of his investigation?

To try to answer this question is a bold undertaking. For since the time of St. Thomas many different answers have been given by great commentators. But the fact that the answer is still a subject of debate today is an indication that the answers that have been given are not satisfying. It is only the encouragement that I have received from my professors at the Gregorian University as well as from my friends at St. Louis University that leads me to present a new solution to the question in this study.

To arrive at certainty in the answer to this question is of great importance for the understanding of St. Thomas' teaching on the nature of theology. For the first question of the Summa has been regarded for centuries as the locus classicus for theologians in investigating the nature of their science. And the results of their investigations have been closely connected with their interpretation of the meaning of sacra doctrina in the Summa of St. Thomas.

It goes without saying that one must know the subject which a teacher is discussing in order to understand properly what he is saying. It is true, however, that sometimes the same things can be said about different subjects, and that even when we do not know with certainty the subject of predication, we can understand several things in what is said which are true, but which may not be the precise thing that is intended.

For example, many things can be said about Sacred Scripture which can also be said about the habit of sacred theology. Scripture makes use of metaphor, for example; so does the habit of sacred theology. But no one will deny that Scripture is something different from the habit of sacred theology. Hence when St. Thomas says that sacred doctrine makes use of metaphor, even if I don't know exactly what he means by sacred doctrine, I can interpret him as saying either that Sacred Scripture makes use of metaphor or the habit of sacred theology makes use of metaphor. Thus while what I think he is saying is true, he may not be saying this at all.

It is clear, then, that for a proper understanding of what St. Thomas is saying in the first question of the Summa we must endeavor to find out with certainty the subject he is talking about. Otherwise although what we interpret him to say may be true, our interpretation may not represent what he is saying.

Hence, if in this study we can succeed not only in presenting a new opinion, but in arriving at certainty as to the subject of predication in the first question of the Summa, this study will be of value as a firm basis for further investigation of Thomas' thought on the nature of theology, as well as on other questions involved in the first question of the Summa. If the conclusion of this study is not accepted as certain, it may still serve further research in so far as it presents at least a probable opinion in this matter.

Our procedure in this study will be as follows: First we shall see what has been said by the commentators on the Summa regarding the meaning of sacra doctrina, taking care not only to state their opinions about its meaning, but also to indicate the methods and procedures they have used in arriving at their interpretations. Secondly, we shall examine what St. Thomas says about doctrina itself as background for our study of the meaning of the term sacra doctrina. Thirdly, we shall investigate the meaning of the term sacra doctrina itself as used in the first question of the Summa, considering not only the text of the Summa itself, but also parallel passages from the Commentary on the Sentences and texts from other works of St. Thomas which might serve to throw light on the term.

Throughout this study it must be clearly borne in mind that our purpose is merely to point out the reality which is signified by the term sacra doctrina and which forms the subject of the first question of the Summa. We are not engaged in determining the nature of this reality. We must be satisfied here with simply putting our finger, as it were, on the object signified by the term sacra doctrina. Its nature will be the subject of later investigation.

10

For anyone not thoroughly familiar with the text of St. Thomas I would suggest a preliminary re-reading of the first question of the Summa, *in which particular care is taken to notice how St. Thomas uses the term* sacra doctrina. *Otherwise it may be difficult to follow the discussion as it is presented.*

I am sincerely grateful to all those who by their help and encouragement have enabled me to do this work: to Fr. C. Boyer, S. J., my director, Fr. F. Pelster, S. J., and Fr. H. Vignon, S. J., all of the Gregorian University; and also to Fr. G. Klubertanz, S. J. and Fr. C. Vollert, S. J. of St. Louis University.

I am deeply grateful also to Professor Étienne Gilson for taking time to read my dissertation and discuss it with me. His encouraging remarks have led me to present it for publication.

In a special way I wish to thank Fr. Yves M.-J. Congar, O.P. for preparing the introduction for this work. He has graciously written it in the form of a letter. My great admiration for Fr. Congar and his work as well as his authority on the subject I treat led me to ask this favor of him. I only hope that my work may prove worthy of the time and energy of those who have been so generous with their help.

LETTER OF INTRODUCTION

By Fr. Yves M.-J. Congar, OP.

Mon Révérend Père,

Vous avez bien voulu me demander de lire votre Thèse et de lui donner éventuellement une sorte d'introduction. Elle n'a pourtant pas besoin de ma présentation, car elle se recommande d'elle même ; encore moins de mon patronage, ayant celui de l'Université Grégorienne, de laquelle elle vous a valu le titre de Docteur. Avec la simplicité que réclame la fraternité du travail théologique, je répondrai pourtant à votre confiance et, puisque vous m'y conviez, je marquerai ici mon accord et les limites de celui-ci.

Accord, en premier lieu, sur votre méthode : celle d'une étude du vocabulaire. J'ai, pour ma part, reçu naguère, à cet égard, de l'enseignement si suggestif du R. P. Chenu, un éveil que le travail personnel a confirmé. On apprend beaucoup de l'étude attentive des mots pour l'intelligence des textes. Nous devons à une telle méthode, encore trop négligée par beaucoup, une grande partie de la précision et du relief qu'a aujourd'hui notre connaissance du Moyen Age, comme des extraordinaires progrès faits en exégèse biblique depuis un quart de siècle.

Accord aussi sur le sens de (sacra) doctrina. Le mot signifie très exactement « enseignement », avec l'ambivalence de l'expression française qui peut désigner, soit (et en premier lieu) l'acte d'enseigner, le processus par lequel un maître éveille une connaisance organiquement structurée dans un esprit, — soit le contenu, la chose ou l'ensemble de choses enseignées, — soit les deux à la fois. Un coup d'oeil jeté sur une feuille où j'avais noté naguère quelques emplois du mot faits par S. Thomas *in actu exercito*, m'a confirmé dans ces convictions [1].

---

(1) Sens actif (acte d'enseigner) *Com. in Ethic.*, I, lect. 1 ; *Sum. theol,*, I-II, q. 34, a. 1 c. ; III, q. 7, a. 7 ; III, q. 42 ; *Quodl.*, II, 6 ; *C. Gent.*, II, 4 fin ; *in Rom.*, c. 1, lect. 5 ; *in 2 Tim.*, c. 4, lect. 1.

A la fois sens actif et sens de contenu (doctrine enseignée) : *Sum. Theol.,*

Il faudrait évidemment pousser plus loin l'enquête. Un vocabulaire relève généralement de tout un milieu ; bien que S. Thomas ait joué un rôle décisif dans la fixation du vocabulaire théologique, l'usage qu'il fait des mots ne saurait être étudié sans référence à des antécédents, à un contexte. Il est probable qu'une enquête faite auprès d'autres témoins n'apporterait rien de discordant, au moins quant au sens général du mot [1]. Mais il n'est pas impossible que S. Thomas en fasse ici un emploi original, où se traduit une option et une synthèse personnelles. Je serais pour ma part, porté à le penser, mais il faudrait, pour l'affirmer, plus que quelques coups de sonde [2]. Le travail vaudrait d'être entrepris et je souhaite qu'il vous tente un jour.

S'il était avéré que l'emploi de *Sacra doctrina* représente, de la part de S. Thomas, une option originale et consciente, on ne pourrait avoir une pleine intelligence de la 1re question de sa *Somme* qu'après avoir étudié l'idée qu'il avait de l'économie totale de l'enseignement chrétien, celui qui procure le salut. A l'intérieur de la grande idée médiévale du caractère hiérarchique de la communication des dons de Dieu [3], on verrait se placer, chacun en son ordre d'autorité et de ministère, le Christ (*De doctrina Christi* : IIIa,

---

II-II, q. 5, a. 3, ad 2 ; III, q. 35, a. 5 ; *In Epist. Pauli*, prol. ; *in 1 Cor.*, c. 3, lect. 2 ; c. 12, lect. 3 ; *in Tit.*, c. 1, lect. 3 ; *Contra impugn.*, c. 2 ; Q. disp. de Caritate, a. 13, Q. disp. de Caritate, a. 13 ad 6.

(1) Pour les Pères, cf. H.-I. MARROU « *Doctrina* » *et* « *Disciplina* » *dans la langue des Pères de l'Eglise*, dans *Bull. Du Cange*, 10 (1934), p. 5-25. On pourrait évidemment ajouter indéfiniment des fiches. En voici une touchant Robert de Melun : « Primus homo ante peccatum sine omni adminiculo doctrinae extrinsecae Creatoris et creaturarum sufficientem habere potuit cognitionem... Post culpam, Sacrae Scripturae eguit doctrina ». *Summa*, I, 1, XIV et XV (cité par A. LANDGRAF, dans *Scholastik,* 1928, p. 31, n.).

(2) Voici le résultat d'un coup de sonde rapide. Il semble bien que dans les considérations de méthode correspondant à la Ire question de la *Somme*, les auteurs antérieurs (par ex. Gilbert de la Porrée, Etienne de Tournai) et ceux du XIIIe siècle (Jean de St. Gilles, Roland de Crémone, O.P., et surtout les Franciscains, S. Bonaventure, Eudes Rigaud, Guillaume de Méliton, R. Bacon, Peckham) emploient *theologia*. Non qu'on ne puisse trouver ici ou là l'expression *doctrina*, mais en passant seulement, non avec cette constance qui, dans la Somme, semble bien dénoncer un propos intentionnel. Pour S. Thomas, *theologia* désigne la discipline qui parle de Dieu ; il y en a deux, une qui relève de la métaphysique, l'autre « quae ad sacram doctrinam pertinet », qui vient et relève de l'enseignement dont la Révélation est la source et la règle.

D'autre part, quand les contemporains de S. Thomas posent la question de la nécessité, celle qui correspond au 1er art. de la *Somme*, ils la posent généralement en termes de nécessité *de la foi*, non d'une *doctrina sacra*. Par ex. Barthélémy de Bologne, contemporain de S. Thomas.

(3) Qui s'appuie évidemment sur Denys. Voir comme typique le texte du concile de Latran de 1215, si « thomiste » avant la lettre : Denzinger, n. 428, et S. THOMAS, *Sum. th.*, II-II, q. 2, a. 6.

q. 42), les Apôtres (cf. in *1 Cor.*, c. 12, lect. 3), l'Eglise (cf. IIª-IIªᵉ, q. 5, a. 3, ad 2), les Docteurs chrétiens, « Sancti » d'abord, maîtres et docteurs ensuite [1]. Il serait très intéressant d'étudier l'idée que S. Thomas s'est faite, et qu'il a vécue avec une telle intégrité, du rôle du docteur chrétien : « Ego hoc vel praecipuum vitae meae officium debere me Deo conscius sum, ut eum omnis sermo meus et sensus loquatur » [2]. Mais il faudrait surtout voir tout cela sous la lumière d'une théologie d'ensemble de l'enseignement, et très spécialement de l'enseignement sacré, *sacra doctrina*. Pour l'enseignement en général, la q. 117, de la 1ª Pars (avec le commentaire de Cajetan), et d'autres textes que vous citez, sont explicites à souhait. S. Thomas voit l'enseignement comme une des grandes formes fondamentales de participation de l'homme au gouvernement du monde par lequel Dieu *meut* la création vers le terme qu'il lui a destiné : plus précisément, une des deux grandes façons dont les hommes coopèrent avec Dieu en agissant sur d'autres hommes : l'enseignement (q. 117) et la génération charnelle (q. 118-119). Cette dualité d'action se retrouve ensuite, par exemple quand il s'agit de savoir comment un homme peut être cause de péché pour un autre homme (« exterius suggerendo...; per generationem ») ; puis, dans l'économie chrétienne de régénération, sous la forme de la loi et de la grâce, dans l'action du Christ, puis des Apôtres, « per modum doctrinae et operationis (vel administrationis sacramentorum) », ou encore dans la double incorporation au Christ, « mentaliter, per fidem ; corporaliter, per sacramenta », etc. [3]. Bref, c'est à l'intérieur d'une forme décisive du grand mouvement par lequel il voit toutes choses, et singulièrement l'homme, revenir à la fin céleste du salut, que S. Thomas situe et comprend la *Doctrina sacra*, l'activité de communication à l'esprit de ce qui concerne la fin et les moyens

---

(1) Voir S. THOMAS, *in 1 Cor.*, c. 12, lect. 3. On manque encore d'une étude sur ce sujet. Voir quelques indications dans R. GUELLUY. *La place des théologiens dans l'Eglise et la société médiévales*, dans *Miscellanea hist. A. De Meyer*, Louvain, 1946, t. I, p. 571-589 ; J. LECLERCQ, *Le magistère du prédicateur au XIIIᵉ siècle*, dans *Arch. Hist. doctr. et litt. du M. A.*, 15 (1946), p. 105-147 ; *L'idéal du théologien au M. A. (Textes inédits)*, dans *Rev. des Sciences relig.*, 21 (1947), p. 121-148.

(2) Texte de S. Hilaire (*De Trin.*, I, 37 : P. L., 10,48) repris à son compte par S. Thomas au début de sa carrière : *C. Gent.*, I, 2. Puis-je renvoyer à un article sur *S. Thomas, serviteur de la vérité*, dans *Vie spirituelle* mars 1937, p. 259-279, où je développe d'ailleurs le point de vue, non proprement du docteur, mais du serviteur ?

(3) *Sum theol.*, I-II, q. 19, a. 5 ad 1. Mon confrère le R. P. A. Motte a attiré mon attention sur plusieurs de ces points.

de notre destinée surnaturelle. On parlerait aujourd'hui du caractère eschatologique et de la valeur « heilsgeschichtlich » de l'enseignement sacré... Il n'est pas douteux que le premier article de la *Somme* ne contienne tout cela et ne mette tout ce qui suit sous le signe de cette finalité.

Ainsi S. Thomas, ne se distinguant en cela de son milieu spirituel que par une plus grande acuité de ses perceptions et une plus grand logique de ses démarches, voyait-il l'histoire terrestre comme remplie par le développement, côte à côte, de deux processus : le premier, de multiplication des hommes par la génération charnelle, qui représentait une part éminente du « processus creaturarum a Deo », l'autre de constitution de la *Societas fidelium* qui est l'Eglise [1], à partir de l'enseignement reçu par révélation des prophètes, du Christ et des Apôtres. *Semen est verbum Dei.* On dirait aussi bien, du point de vue de l'oeuvre de l'intelligence : le premier, de conquête scientifique par l'esprit de l'homme ; le second, de soumission de ce même esprit à la foi. Mais le puissant idéal d'unité dont vivait le Moyen Age ne pouvait admettre que deux mondes se dévelopassent côte à côte sans se ramener à l'unité par une subordination de l'un à l'autre. D'où, au plan politique, la grande lutte du Sacerdoce et de l'Empire ; d'où, au plan de la pensée, la grande ambition d'un savoir total architectoniquement polarisé et réglé par la foi. Certes, la synthèse bonaventurienne de la *Reductio artium ad theologiam* est profondément différente, quant à ses options épistémologiques et finalement métaphysiques, de la synthèse thomiste : chacune, en son genre, est totale et pure, chacune honore l'idéal qui les commande toutes deux. Il s'agit, au fond, d'assumer dans le mouvement de retour à Dieu, tout le développement du Monde et, au plan des activités de l'esprit, tout enseignement, toute *doctrina* valable, sous la régulation et au service de cette *doctrina* souveraine et sacrée qui, venue de Dieu lui-même, nous renseigne sur la fin dernière de toutes choses [2].

---

(1) Voir A. Darquennes, S.J. *La définition de l'Eglise d'après S. Thomas d'Aquin*, dans *L'organisation corporative du Moyen Age à la fin de l'Ancien Régime. Et. prés. à la Commission intern. pour l'Hist. des Assemblées d'Etats*, t. VIII, Louvain, 1943, p. 1-52. Voir aussi mes *Jalons pour une Théologie du Laïcat*.

(2) Cette idée, qui semble bien être celle de S. Thomas, est suggérée de façon remarquable dans ce texte de son contemporain franciscain Barthélémy de Bologne : « Constat quod ordini motorum respondet ex aequali ordo finium per aliquid intermedium utrique extremorum proportionatum. Verbi gratia : grammaticus est inter doctores liberales infimus doctor sive motor intellectus, et sic

J'ai dit que j'exprimerais les limites de mon accord. J'entendais par là essentiellement les limites de ma compétence. J'ai passablement étudié ces questions, mais avant 1939 ... Depuis, après six ans de guerre et de captivité, je me suis trouvé engagé dans d'autres travaux qui ne m'ont pas même laissé le temps de réaliser le projet, un moment caressé, de reprendre l'article « Théologie » du *Dictionnaire de Théologie catholique* que le Directeur de celui-ci, Mgr. Amann, a écourté des deux cinquièmes (exactement de 3.987 lignes sur 11.506) ... Il m'est donc impossible d'engager, sur tous les points que vous touchez, une adhésion motivée dont vous n'avez d'ailleurs nul besoin ...

D'une façon générale, je crois qu'il faut éviter, lorsqu'on interprète S. Thomas, de trop systématiser, même à partir d'une perception vraie. Je me demande si ce n'est pas ce qu'a un peu fait M. Gilson à propos du *revelabile* de l'article 3. Pour ma part, je donnerais à cette expression le sens plus simple de : tout ce qui est susceptible d'apparaître à l'esprit sous la lumière de la révélation divine : étant entendu que S. Thomas a contribué de façon décisive à faire passer le mot *Revelatio* du sens fort large et un peu vague qu'il avait alors, à la désignation de la Révélation historique, celle de l'économie chrétienne, « apostolis et prophetis facta, qui canonicos libros scripserunt » (a. 8, ad 2)[1]. C'est pourquoi, pour le dire en passant, si le sens que vous avez restitué à *doctrina* — à savoir celui d'enseignement (scientifique) engendrant un habitus (scientifique) — se prêterait à envisager et à élaborer une théorie du développement dogmatique dans l'enseignement de l'Eglise, on voit mal comment la pensée de S. Thomas admettrait l'idée,

---

movet ipsum intellectum ad quendam finem infimum in genere finium doctrinalium, sc. ad notitiam grammaticalium ; et hoc facit per quoddam intermedium praedicto motori et fini proportionatum ; et hoc est lumen grammaticalium documentorum et regularum. Logicus vero, qui est superior doctor et motor intellectus, etiam movet ad finem altiorem. sc. qui scientia recte ratiocinandi ... Idem intelligendum est per simile de medico naturali, mathematico et theologo omnium doctorum supremo tam triviali quam quadrivialium. Sicut ergo theologus est doctor altissimus, ita etiam habitus scientiae ad quem movet intellectum ... » *Quaest. de fide*, q. 4 (M. MÜCKSHOFF. *Die Quaestiones disp. de fide des Bartholomäus von Bologna, O.F.M.* (*Beitr. z. Gesch. d. Philos. u. Theol. d. Mitt.*, XXIV/4). Munster, 1940, p. 73).

(1) Voir J. DE GHELLINCK. *Pour l'histoire du mot revelare*, dans *Rech. de Science religieuse* 6 (1916), p. 149-157 ; J. DE GUIBERT. *Pour une étude des « loca parallela » de S. Thomas*, dans *Bull. de Littér. ecclés.*, 1914, p. 472 s. (reproduit dans *Les doublets de S. Thomas d'Aquin* ... Paris 1926, p. 55 s.). Le changement signalé entre les textes parallèles des *Sentences* et de la *Somme* est patent et remarquable. Il dénonce une prise de conscience très ferme du statut de l'économie chrétienne.

17

tenue encore par certains au Moyen Age, d'une croissance *de la Révélation* dans l'enseignement de l'Eglise. Mais, très sagement, vous vous en êtes tenu à une exégèse de la question et n'avez pas cherché à déborder les perspectives où vous mettait votre texte.

Pourtant, après avoir commenté des textes et fait ainsi, au sens historique du mot, oeuvre de « Scolastique », le théologien se doit de penser directement *des problèmes*. En cette seconde étape de son travail, les maîtres les plus sûrs, comme est S. Thomas pour nous, ne sont plus pour lui à proprement parler des normes, mais plutôt des initiateurs. C'est encore et toujours avec eux, grâce à eux, qu'on travaille; on ne leur demande plus de fournir, tel quel et de façon normative, tout le contenu de la pensée. Il me reste à souhaiter qu'après avoir si bien parcouru la première étape, vous fournissiez aussi la seconde, et qu'elle soit pour vous longue et féconde.

Le Saulchoir, 13 Novembre 1950.

fr. Yves M.-J. CONGAR O.P.

18

CHAPTER ONE

INTERPRETATIONS
OF THE MEANING OF SACRA DOCTRINA

CAJETAN

The first significant commentary on the meaning of the word *sacra doctrina* in the first question of the *Summa Theologica* of St. Thomas is given us by Cardinal Cajetan (1469-1534), in his *Commentarii in Summam Theologiae s. Thomae Aquinatis, Pars I*, which he completed in the year 1508 [1].

Cardinal Cajetan's interpretation is based not only on the immediate context of the first question of the *Summa*, but on the whole *Summa* and his superior knowledge of the works of St. Thomas.

Commenting on the first article he says that *sacra doctrina* is to be understood in the sense of knowledge either formally or virtually revealed by God, having the character of discipline and doctrine, and abstracting from whether it is knowledge which is faith or knowledge which is science.

He has arrived at this conclusion from a consideration not of the nominal meaning of the word, but of the incongruities which follow from trying to understand the term as signifying either faith or theology. For if it is understood as signifying faith, then St. Thomas would be treating the same question twice in the *Summa*, a thing which would be incongruous in such a work.

(1) For the various editions of Cajetan's works see A. MICHELITSCH, *Thomistenschriften 2. Kommentatoren zur Summa Theologiae d. Thomas von Aquin.* Graz und Wien : Styria, 1924, pp. 302. The text which I am using is found in the Leonine edition of the works of St. Thomas, in which the *Summa Theologica* together with Cajetan's commentary appears beginning with Tome IV.

It would also follow that the term is used equivocally in the following articles where it certainly does not signify faith. This is also considered incongruous.

If, however, the term is understood in the sense of theology, then it would follow that faith without theology would not be sufficient for salvation ; which is false. The logic of this reasoning, however, is clear because in the text it is said that this doctrine is necessary for salvation. But the falsity of the conclusion itself is evident and is proven from the reason which is assigned in the text : namely, that man can direct his intentions and actions to his supernatural end through his knowledge of faith [1].

Since *sacra doctrina* cannot signify either faith or theology, it must then signify knowledge either formally or virtually revealed by God, having the character of discipline and doctrine, but considered as abstracted from the differences specifying this knowledge as faith or science. For the knowledge which we need for salvation, since it is received by man from God his teacher, is doctrine and discipline, according to the words of St. John IV, 45 : « Everyone who heareth the Father and learneth cometh to me ». This doctrine and discipline here in the first article is said to be necessary for salvation. Knowledge of this kind, because it is a revealed discipline, abstracts from the differences which specify it as faith or science, and from the differences which specify it as formally or virtually revealed. Hence it follows that in this text where the question is about a revealed doctrine other than the physical disciplines, the concept *sacra doctrina* does not legitimately include these differences [2].

(1) CAJETAN, *Comm. in Sum.*, in Partem I, q. 1, art. 1 (ed. Leon., t. IV, p. 7a-7b) :
— V. Circa hanc conclusionem dubium statim occurrit, quid intelligatur hic nomine *sacrae doctrinae* seu disciplinae. Aut enim intelligitur fides, aut theologia. Si fides, sequuntur duo inconvenientia. Primum est, quod idem bis quaereretur : nam in IIa IIae, qu. 11, art. 3, quaeretur an credere aliquid supernaturale sit necessarium ad salutem. Secundum est, quod aequivoce sumitur sacra doctrina in hoc et in sequentibus articulis : nam constat quod in eis non sumitur pro fide. — Si theologia, sequeretur quod fides absque theologia non sufficeret ad salutem hominis : quod est falsum. Sequela patet : quia in littera dicitur quod illa doctrina est necessaria ad salutem humanam. Falsitas vero consequentis et ex se patet, et ex ratione in littera assignata convincitur : quia scilicet homo potest intentiones et actiones suas per fidei cognitionem in finem supernaturalem dirigere.
(2) *Ibid.*, (ed. Leon., IV, p. 7b) :
— VI. Ad hoc dicendum est quod sacra doctrina neque sumitur pro fide, ut distinguitur contra theologiam ; neque pro theologia, ut distinguitur contra fidem : sed sumitur pro cognitione a Deo revelata, sive formaliter, sive virtualiter, ut

Cajetan then proceeds to justify the correctness of this understanding of the term. First of all, this interpretation avoids the incongruities which follow from interpreting the word as signifying faith. For thus the question in the first article is formally different from the question found later on in the IIa-IIae; for here there in question of doctrine, there of faith. Moreover, the term as used here and in the second article would be univocal.

Secondly, — this interpretation avoids the incongruity which follows from interpreting the word as signifying theology. For it does not follow from this interpretation that theology as distinguished from faith is necessary, but that theology, according as it abstracts from faith and science, is necessary for salvation. Nor can one argue in this way: faith suffices, therefore theology is not required. This argument is invalid because theology as it is understood here is included in faith in a manner similar to the way that animal is included in man; and also because this science, according to Augustine, not only nourishes, defends, and strengthens faith, but gives birth to it. And this is true in regard to the object of faith *(credibilia)*. For although faith comes from God infusing into us the inclination to believe, the determination of what is to be believed comes from hearing the word of Christ, *ex auditu per verbum Christi.* And thus it is that theology is included in faith as giving birth to it.

Finally, if one should infer from this that every adult believer who explicitly believes is a theologian, it must be said that this is not true absolutely, but only in a certain sense, in so far as a believer participates theology in knowing its principles [1].

habet rationem disciplinae et doctrinae, abstrahendo a ratione crediti et sciti. Cognitio enim qua egemus ad salutem, prout a Deo docente in homine suscipitur, doctrina est et disciplina, iuxta illud Ioan. VI [45]. *Omnis qui audivit a Patre et didicit, venit ad me.* Et de hac dicitur in conclusione hac, quod est necessaria ad salutem. Et quoniam cognitio huiusmodi, ut disciplina est revelata, abstrahit a ratione credendi et sciendi; et a ratione revelati formaliter, id est in seipso, et virtualiter, id est in suis principiis: ideo hoc in loco, ubi de doctrina revelata praeter physicas disciplinas quaeritur, ad nullum horum licet determinate descendere.

(1) *Ibid.,* (ed. Leon., IV, p. 7b):
— Et sic aliud formaliter quaeritur hic, et aliud quaeretur inferius in IIa-IIae: quia hic de *doctrina,* ibi de *credere.* Et univoce sumitur hic sacra doctrina et in sequenti articulo. Nec sequitur quod theologia ut distinguitur contra fidem, sit necessaria; sed quod theologia ut abstrahit a fide et scientia, sit necessaria ad salutem; quod constat esse verum, propter rationem in littera assignatam. Nec valet: *fides sufficit; ergo theologia non requiritur:* tum quoniam in fide clauditur theologia, ut hic sumitur, sicut animal in homine; tum quoniam scientia

It is very interesting to watch Cajetan wrestle with this concept of sacred doctrine. The suppositions in his discussion are at least two: 1) that the term is not equivocal in this article and in the following articles; and 2) that St. Thomas would not formally treat the same question twice in the same work. A third quasi-supposition is that *sacra doctrina* has only three possible meanings; namely, faith, theology, and knowledge revealed by God but considered as abstracted from the differences specifying it as faith or theology. We say quasi-supposition, because Cajetan does not say he is giving a complete enumeration of the possible meanings of *sacra doctrina*. After rejecting the meanings of faith and theology, he accepts the third meaning, because, as he says, the knowledge needed for salvation is doctrine and discipline and because knowledge of this kind abstracts from the differences specifying it as faith or theology.

But he does not tell us WHY knowledge of this kind, i. e. doctrine and discipline, makes such abstraction.

We notice, too, that in his examination of the correctness of his interpretation, Cajetan uses the word theology in two different senses. First, he uses it as signifying theological science, as it is distinguished from faith; thus theology is not necessary for salvation. Secondly, he (consciously or unconsciously) uses it as synonymous with *sacra doctrina*, when he speaks of theology as it abstracts from faith and science; thus theology is required for salvation, because theology in this sense is included in faith and gives birth to faith. Theology is included in faith in the way that animal is included in man, i. e. as genus is included in species. And, moreover, it is included in faith in another manner, namely, in so far as it gives birth to faith.

Here Cajetan becomes obscure and one is tempted to think that he is confusing the two meanings he has given to theology. What I think he is saying is that theology (?) is included in faith in so far as the object of faith *(credibilia)* being explicitly represented in this knowledge generates explicit faith in definite things

haec, apud Augustinum XIV *de Trinitate*, non solum nutrit, defendit et roborat fidem, sed gignit eandem. Et vere sic est ex parte credibilium. Fides enim, licet sit a Deo infundente inclinationem ad credendum, est tamen ex auditu per verbum Christi quoad credibilia, ut *ad Rom.* X habetur, in littera, et a S. Thoma. Et si inferatur: *ergo quilibet fidelis adultus explicite credens etc. est theologus:* dicendum est quod non simpliciter: sed particeps est theologiae secundum quid etc., scilicet secundum principia etc.

to be believed; for this « explicitation » of faith is caused by hearing the word of Christ.

What is clear is that Cajetan interprets *sacra doctrina* to signify, after the manner of genus, knowledge revealed by God, the species of which are faith and theological science.

Commenting on the second article of the *Summa*, Cajetan indicates that the term *sacra doctrina* is here used in the same sense as it was in the first article, but modified by the context.

— In titulo huius secundi articuli, nota duos terminos: primo ly *scientia;* secundo ly *sacra doctrina.* Scientia enim sumitur hic proprie, ut est intellectualis virtus (VI Ethic.*), et habitus conclusionum per demonstrationem acquisibilis ex principiis. Et quoniam talia sunt subiecta qualia permittuntur a praedicatis, consequens est quod ly *sacra doctrina* sumatur hic pro doctrina revelata *ut est conclusionum.* Neque enim sumitur pro tota (quoniam stultum videtur quaerere an tota cognitio, claudens in se principia et conclusiones, sit scientia, cum constet principiorum non esse scientiam): sed pro ipsa absolute, ut in primo articulo*, adiuncto respectu ad conclusiones. Ita quod sensus quaestionis est: An sacra doctrina, quam probavimus necessariam, quoad conclusiones suas habet rationem scientiae; an non, sed opinionis etc. Et sic idem omnino est subiectum quaestionis et conclusionis responsivae: et quaestiones aequantur vere scitis, iuxta doctrinam II *Poster**[1].

The principle which Cajetan here uses to determine the sense of *sacra doctrina*, the subject of this question, is the following: *talia sunt subiecta qualia permittuntur a praedicatis.* He first determines the meaning of the predicate term *scientia. Scientia enim sumitur hic proprie, ut est intellectualis virtus*..., *et habitus conclusionum per demonstrationem acquisibilis ex principiis.* For this interpretation he gives no reason. He then applies the principle: *talis sunt subiecta qualia permittuntur a praedicatis,* and concludes: *consequens est quod ly sacra doctrina sumatur hic pro doctrina revelata ut est conclusionum. Neque enim sumitur pro tota*..., *sed pro ipsa absolute, ut in primo articulo, adiuncto respectu ad conclusiones.*

To illustrate his procedure let us consider a similar question, whether animal is rational being. As the subject animal in this question must be such as the predicate will permit, it is clear that animal here is not taken to mean all that is animal but animal according to one of its subjective parts. This does not mean that

(1) *Ibid.,* art. 2 (ed. Leon., IV, p. 9a).

the comprehension of the term animal is changed to fit the predicate, but that the extension of the term is limited by the predicate or by the context.

We grant that the principle and the procedure he uses is sound. But we note first of all that he gives no reason for his interpretation of *scientia* in this article; he may be right, of course, but we would like to see his reasons for such an interpretation. And secondly, we notice some difficulty in taking the predicate term to signify the intellectual virtue of science if the subject of which it is predicated *in recto* is *cognitio*, for then the affirmative response to this question must imply: *aliqua cognitio est virtus intellectualis*. We do not deny that this sort of predication can be made, in so far as a cause can be predicated of its effect or vice-versa, but we wonder if this is the type of predication that St. Thomas is making use of in this article.

Commenting on the third article Cajetan states quite simply that *sacra doctrina* here means *tota scientia theologica*.

— In titulo nota duos terminos, scilicet subiectum et praedicatum: ly enim *sacra doctrina* sumitur pro tota scientia theologica; ly *una* supponit pro unitate speciei specialissimae ... [1].

We merely note that this does not necessarily imply any change in the signification of the term *sacra doctrina* itself. For a generic term may be qualified by its context with the result that the term *together with* its context signifies the object after the manner of species. Moreover, in view of the fact that Cajetan considers it incongruous that the term should be used equivocally in the first and the following articles, I think it is quite safe to accept the term *sacra doctrina* in the same sense as in the preceding articles, with its sense however so modified by the context that together with its context it comes to mean *tota scientia theologica*.

After this third article Cajetan does no more commenting on the term *sacra doctrina*. He has treated of the relation of the meaning of this term to that of the terms faith and theology. But he does not discuss its relation to Sacred Scripture. In fact, commenting on the tenth article of this question, he freely substitutes the term *sacra doctrina* for the expression *Sacra Scriptura*. He does not explain his reasons for using *sacra doctrina* in this way. But in

(1) *Ibid.*, art. 3, (ed. Leon., IV, p. 12).

so far as Scripture can be called knowledge revealed by God, Scripture can be called *sacra doctrina*, even though *sacra doctrina* itself according to him prescinds from the specification of this knowledge as faith or theology. Specification here again can be derived from the context.

Cajetan therefore holds for the univocity of the term *sacra doctrina* throughout the first question of the *Summa*. Its meaning is knowledge revealed by God prescinding from the specification of this knowledge as faith or theology, as formally or virtually revealed. The context, however, in which it is used may specify this knowledge as faith or theology.

Among the modern commentators on St. Thomas there is no one of note who follows Cajetan's interpretation.

SYLVIUS

Like Cajetan, Francis Sylvius (1581-1649) maintains that the term *sacra doctrina* has the same sense throughout the first question of the *Summa*. For him, however, it does not mean a revealed knowledge abstracted from faith and theology, but theology itself which he describes as an habitual or actual knowledge about God and divine things proceeding from the articles of faith as principles of this knowledge [1].

The four arguments which Sylvius gives for his opinion may be summarized as follows:

1. St. Thomas here (art. 1) is speaking about that doctrine which he investigates in the first question. But what he investigates is not the character and

---

(1) FRANCISCUS SYLVIUS, *Opera omnia*. Tomi VI. - Tome I: *Commentarii in Totam Primam Partem S. Thomae Aquinatis Doctoris Angelici et Communis*. Antuerpiae, 1714: — qu. 1, art. 1, Quaeritur 1. (The Commentary on The First Part of the *Summa* was first published in 1630).

Sylvius' understanding of the word theology may be gathered from the following texts:

« Non quaeritur de Theologia prout est in methodum redacta, sive per S. Ioannem Damascenum, sive per Petrum Lombardum, qui vulgo Magister sententiarum dicitur; sive per B. Thomam Aquinatem: sed generaliter prout importat cognitionem de Deo rebusque divinis innixam principiis seu articulis fidei ».
                    (qu. 1, art. 1. Quaeritur 3).

« Denique, Theologia est habitus; et non est intellectus principiorum, cum sit conclusionibus; neque est opinio, cum sit habitus certus: neque fides, quia haec et innititur testimonio dicentis, et versatur articulos fidei qui sunt principia Theologiae; neque etiam est prudentia, quia haec versatur circa singularia agibilia: ergo a sufficienti divisione, est scientia ».
                    (qu. 1, art. 2. Ratio Tertia).

extension of sacred doctrine considered in general and in the abstract; he is investigating the character and extension of theology. Hence he is speaking about theology.

2. In the first article St. Thomas is talking about the same sacred doctrine which in the following articles is called science, one science, more exalted than all other sciences etc. But in those articles he is talking about theology. Therefore also in the first article.

3. St. Thomas calls sacred doctrine that doctrine which proceeds from revealed principles (art. 2) and which has for its principles the articles of faith (art. 7 and 8). But only theology proceeds in this way. Therefore by sacred doctrine he understands theology.

4. In the *Commentary* St. Thomas shows the necessity of some doctrine which proceeds from principles of faith, and which commands all other sciences, etc. But this can only be theology [1].

These arguments are really concerned only with the meaning of sacred doctrine in the first article of the *Summa*. They suppose, however, that the term is used in the same sense throughout the first question.

Sylvius, moreover, seems to be unaware of any possible distinction between the teaching of science and science itself, both

(1) *Ibid.*, qu. 1, art. 1, Quaeritur 1 : — Primo, quia de ea doctrina hic loquitur, de qua huius q. prooemio dixit necessarium esse, primo investigare de ipsa Sacra Doctrina qualis sit et ad quae se extendat; non investigat autem hac prima quaestione de Sacra Doctrina abstractim et in genere, qualis sit et ad quae se extendat, sed de Theologia : ergo non loquitur de Doctrina Sacra abstractim a fide et Theologia, sed de Theologia.

Secundo, dum hoc art. 1 concludit praeter Philosophicas disciplinas necessarium esse; Sacram Doctrinam per revelationem haberi; loquitur de ea Sacra Doctrina, quam art. 2 resolvit esse scientiam, eamque unam, art. 3 et omnibus aliis scientiis digniorem art. 5 et argumentativam, art. 8. Manifestum est autem, quod in istis articulis loquatur de Theologia; ergo et in hoc primo artic. Maior patet, tum ex articulorum contextu, tum ex praefantis q. prooemio, in qua sic praefatur : Circa quae quaerenda decem. Primo, de necessitate huius doctrinae. Secundo, utrum sit scientia. Tertio, utrum sit una vel plures, ... Ubi clarum est ipsum semper de eadem Sacra Doctrina mentionem facere. Minor facile probari potest, partim quia neque fides, neque Sacra Doctrina abstractim et in genere considerata, est secundum se scientia, eaque una, argumentativa, et omnibus aliis scientiis praestantior : partim quia quaestionis et articulorum series evidenter ostendit de Theologia eiusque subiecto hic disseri.

.....

Tertio, Doctrinam Sacram vocat B. Thomas, eam quae procedit ex principiis revelatis art. 2. et quae pro suis principiis habet articulos fidei, art. 7 et 8 conformiter iis, quae scribit opusculo 70, q. 3, art. 2. Atqui sola Theologia procedit ex principiis revelatis, habetque articulos fidei pro suis principiis : ergo per Sacram Doctrinam intelligit Theologiam.

Quarto, initio primo l. sent. ubi eumdem articulum proposuit, quem hic proponit, resolvit oportere esse aliquam doctrinam, quae ex fidei principiis procedat, eamque dicit imperare omnibus aliis scientiis, et uti his, quae in aliis traduntur : haec autem nulli conveniunt, nisi Theologiae.

26

of which proceed from principles. However, as we can judge the validity of his arguments only after studying the text itself of St. Thomas, I will not attempt to evaluate his arguments here, but merely point out one of the main difficulties involved in this interpretation.

To conclude that *sacra doctrina* means theology involves understanding St. Thomas to say that theology is necessary for salvation. For St. Thomas devotes the first article of the *Summa* to the demonstration of the necessity of *sacra doctrina* for salvation.

Sylvius recognizes this difficulty and proceeds to solve it as follows : Although theology in its entire perfection is not necessary for all men, nevertheless it is necessary according to some one of its parts in order that man may know the supernatural end to which he is ordered. For this supernatural end does not become known to men without theology.

He then gives two arguments to show that the supernatural end of man does not become known without theology : 1) Even though the supernatural end of man is known only through faith, these articles of faith which man believes are the principles of theology. But the knowledge of the principles of theology is the first part of theology. And hence the supernatural end of man cannot become known without theology. 2) Moreover, in order that our supernatural end as well as other articles of faith become known to men, some instruction is necessary, as St. Paul tells us that faith comes from hearing. But men cannot be taught the mysteries of faith except by those who possess theology, or at least participate it in some degree. Hence the necessity of theology [1].

(1) *Ibid.* — Ad argumentum initio allatum RESP. quamvis Theologia secundum totam suam latitudinem et perfectionem non sit unicuique necessaria ; ex aliqua tamen sui parte omnibus est necessaria ; ad praecognoscendum finem supernaturalem, in quem homo ordinatur ; qui finis, etsi multis innotescat, qui Theologi non sunt, veluti rusticis et aliis hominibus tum illiteratis, tum ratiocinationum Theologicarum imperitis ; non tamen innotescit absque Theologia.

Primo, quia Theologia non solum est notitia conclusionum Theologicarum, sed etiam complectitur notitiam articulorum fidei, qui sunt principia doctrinae Theologicae, horum autem articulorum notitia non habetur nisi per fidem ; et propterea, dum finis supernaturalis innotescit per fidem, non innotescit absque Theologia, sed per cognitionem principiorum Theologicorum, quae cognitio est prima pars Theologiae.

Secundo, quia ut Deus quatenus est finis supernaturalis, et alii articuli fidei hominibus innotescant, necesse est aliquam doctrinam sive instructionem exterius adhiberi ; nam iuxta Apostolum ad Rom. 10, *fides est ex auditu* ; non possunt autem doceri mysteria fidei, ne quidem ruditer et imperfecte, nisi per eos qui vel doctrinam Theologicam callent, vel saltem aliquid de ea participant. Quapropter quod in argumento dicebatur, multos consequi salutem sine adiumento Theolo-

Actually what Sylvius is proving here is the necessity of faith·
And although faith is in a certain sense a part of theology, it
would be very unusual for any theologian to speak of the necessity of theology and mean by that the necessity only of faith. Moreover, the articles of faith are known as principles of theology
only when conclusions also are known which follow from these
articles. When they are known merely in themselves, they are not
known as principles of theology. Hence although men who know
merely the articles of faith can be said to know part of theology,
they do not know it in its quality as part of theology. They can
be saved without knowing the articles of faith as principles of
theology.

Finally, the argument for the necessity of theology from its
necessity in those who teach the faith appears to be entirely for-
eign to Thomas' discussion of the necessity of sacred doctrine.

In brief, we can say that the distinctions and arguments which
Sylvius is forced to make use of to sustain his position are not
well grounded in the text of St. Thomas. This leads us to suspect
that St. Thomas is not treating of the necessity of theology in the
first article of the *Summa*, and that therefore *sacra doctrina* may
demand an interpretation different from that of Sylvius.

Among the more modern theologians who follow Sylvius' opinion in this controversy, we may name Fr. Billuart, O.P. [1], and Fr.
Sertillanges, O.P. [2] Fr. Billuart, moreover, believes that the opinion
of Sylvius is the same as that of John of St. Thomas [3]. This is
not true, as we shall see. I mention Fr. Sertillanges as a disciple

---

giae; negandum est: quamvis enim multi eam consequantur, qui absolute non
sunt Theologi: non tamen consequuntur sine adiumento Theologiae eorum,
qui ipsos instruunt, neque sine lumine fidei, quod ad Theologiam pertinet tamquam notificans eius principia.

Si dicas, hinc sequi parentes et patrinos, qui suos filios aliquando sic instruunt de articulis fidei, ut illi filii nullos audiant vel Doctores vel Praedicato-
res; esse Theologos; RESP. non sequi, quod sint absolute Theologi, sed bene
quod aliquid de vera Theologia participent. Ad absolutam enim denominationem
requiritur, quod forma denominans perfecte insit, et non sufficit qualiscumque
eius participatio.

(1) C. R. BILLUART, O.P., *Summa Sancti Thomae Hodiernis Academiarum
Moribus Accommodata.* Parisiis-Lugduni: Lecoffre, 1878. Tomus I. Dissertatio
Prooemialis, art. 2, p. 4.

(2) A. D. SERTILLANGES, O.P., *Saint Thomas d'Aquin. Somme théologique.
Dieu.* Tome I. Traduction française. 3e édition. Paris-Tournai-Rome: Desclée et
Cie., 1925, pp. 372; cf. Introd., pp. 17-18.

(3) *Loc. cit.*, art. 2, p. 4: Joannes a S. Thoma, Sylvius et plures alii e contra contendunt S. Thomam per sacram doctrinam in hoc primo articulo intelligere
theologiam proprie sumptam. ...

of Sylvius in this matter, because like Sylvius he considers the first question of the *Summa* to be concerned with one thing, namely theology, and that the different terms used by St. Thomas merely indicate different aspects of theology.

JOHN OF ST. THOMAS

John of St. Thomas (1589-1644) is the first of the great commentators on the *Summa* to deny the univocity of the term *sacra doctrina* in the first question [1]. For him the term has two senses. Its first meaning is any sort of knowledge, even probable knowledge, derived by reasoning from revealed truths. Its second meaning is certain knowledge deduced scientifically from formally revealed truths; in this sense he considers it the same as theology [2].

The first sense of *sacra doctrina* is referred to as theological doctrine or theology as doctrine. The term used in this sense is more universal than the term theological science. For it includes also probable knowledge or opinions about theological matters, which do not enter the formal unity of theological science, even though they are materially connected with it. For probable reasonings about theological matters generate a habit which in itself is distinct from the habit of theological science. Yet such reasonings are admitted into this science in a way similar to the way in which demonstrations proceeding from purely natural principles are admitted in this science. Although extraneous to theological science, they form a material unity with it.

Thus *sacra doctrina* meaning theological doctrine is more generic in its signification that the term theological science. For theological science includes only those truths which are certainly

(1) IOANNES a S. THOMA, *Cursus Theologicus*, III Tom. Parisiis-Tornaci-Romae: Desclée et Sociorum, 1931: Tom. I. In Quaestionem I Primae Partis, Disp. II, art. 1, pp. 347-348. (Tome I was first published in 1637).

(2) *Ibid.*, p. 348: — Sic ergo comparantur haec tria, fides, theologia, doctrina sacra, quod fides dicit cognitionem circa res divinas, ut immediate revelatas obscure; et sic praebet principia theologiae, et comparatur ad ipsam sicut lumen principiorum ad scientias naturales. Theologia autem est cognitio scientifica, seu certa, procedens ex formaliter revelatis, et inferens ea quae mediate et virtualiter revelata dicuntur, tamquam deducta, et connexa cum revelatis formaliter. Sacra autem doctrina dicit quamcumque cognitionem probativam ex revelatis a Deo, etiam probabiliter, quamvis communi usu loquentium sumatur pro doctrina probativa certo et scientifice: et sic est idem quod theologia.

and scientifically deduced from revealed principles or from principles subordinated to or deduced from revealed principles [1].

John of St. Thomas understands the term *sacra doctrina* in the first article of the *Summa* to mean theological doctrine, as explained above. The reason why the term must here mean theological doctrine and not theological science is that St. Thomas will prove in the second article that *sacra doctrina* is science, and he must not suppose what he is going to prove later.

However, it is clear that *doctrina* here means knowledge pertaining to theological science. For St. Thomas already speaks of this doctrine as science in this first article. Moreover, he would otherwise be forced to pass over the problem of the necessity of theology in a question where he is expressly dealing whith theology, and to treat of the necessity of faith which he will treat later in its proper place [2].

The term *sacra doctrina* as used in articles two to seven inclusive of the *Summa* is understood by John of St. Thomas to mean

(1) *Ibid.*, art. 7, p. 374 : — Loquimur de scientia theologica, et non solum de doctrina ; nam in doctrina theologica possunt etiam comprehendi discursus aliqui probabiles et opinativi circa materias theologicas : quos certum est de se distinctum habitum a scientia theologica generare, quia nec evidentes sunt nec certi. Unde multo magis distinguitur theologia ab aliis habitibus opinativis circa alias materias: quia et incerti sunt, et doctrinam theologicam non attingunt. Quare opiniones quae in aliqua scientia versantur, nunquam constituunt unam rationem formalem cum tali scientia, sed aggregantur illi materialiter. Similiter demonstrationes, si quae fiunt in progressu huius scientiae ex solis et meris principiis naturalibus, sine subordinatione et deductione ex revelatis : tales demonstrationes non pertinent ad habitum theologicum, sed ut extraneae in hac scientia admittuntur. Quare solum loquimur de habitu theologico, prout comprehendit veritates scientifice et certo deductas ex principiis revelatis, vel per subordinationem ad illa. Ubi etiam distinguitur theologia a fide : quia fides praebet principia, theologia autem deducit conclusiones ex illa. Et sic distinguitur a fide sicut habitus scientiae ab habitu principiorum in naturalibus.

(2) *Ibid.*, art. 1, p. 348 : — Ex his elicies, quid nomine sacrae doctrinae intelligat D. Thomas articulo primo, cum inquirit an sit necessaria praeter philosophicas disciplinas. Intelligit enim nomine doctrinae sacrae cognitionem probativam, et illativam conclusionum ex creditis per fidem ; sed nomine doctrinae eam nominat, non scientiae seu theologiae, quia postea de ipsa probatus est quod sit scientia (in art. 2). Unde non debebat supponere, quod postea debebat inquirere ; sed nomine generico doctrinae usus est, ut universaliori modo probaret necessitatem theologiae ex genere suo. Quod vero nomine doctrinae intellexerit cognitionem pertinentem ad theologiam, constat : tum quia eam doctrinam quam dicit necessariam, appellat scientiam in argumento *Sed contra*, ubi dicit « et aliam scientiam esse divinitus inspiratam », et (in solutione ad 2, ibi) « de eisdem rebus aliam scientiam tractare secundum quod cognoscuntur lumine divinae revelationis » : tum quia alias diminutus fuisset D. Thomas in quaestione in qua agit de theologia, et non de fide, nec de aliquo abstrahente a fide et theologia, praetermittere necessitatem theologiae, et agere de necessiate fidei de qua acturus est suo loco (id est, II-II, q. 2, art. 3).

30

theological science. He speaks of theological science sometimes as a habit of knowledge, sometimes simply as knowledge, a knowledge which is certainly and scientifically derived from revealed truths. Thus *sacra doctrina* is theological science in the true and proper sense of the word science [1].

For this meaning of the term *sacra doctrina* he reserves the word *theologia;* for when he speaks of theological doctrine as theology, he qualifies it by saying *theologia ut doctrina* or simply *sacra doctrina*. Hence the deliberate consistency with which he uses the term *theologia* in his commentary on articles two to seven is a sufficient indication that in these articles he understands *sacra doctrina* as theological science [2].

But when he comes to comment on articles eight and nine, we find that the term *sacra doctrina* appears again and is understood as theological doctrine, no doubt because there is question of knowledge which is not in every case scientific [3].

John of St. Thomas does not use *sacra doctrina* in the sense of Sacred Scripture. For Sacred Scripture is not *sacra doctrina;* it is the first of the theological places [4].

It is important, I think, to see how John of St. Thomas arrives at his interpretation of the term *doctrina,* because from this he proceeds to interpret the meaning of the term *sacra doctrina*. He says that by the word *doctrina* is understood any probative knowledge, as is said in the *Posterior Analytics* and explained by St. Thomas. In the teacher it is called doctrine; in the disciple, discipline. Hence what is required by the notion of probative knowledge is required by the notion of doctrine: that is, something by way of principle from which inference or proof is made, and something by way of conclusion derived or proven. Hence (he continues) it is clear that by the word sacred doctrine is understood knowledge derived by reasoning from revealed truths. For this is sacred knowledge. And so by the word sacred doctrine is meant what is proven through revealed knowledge, whether the proof is probable or scientific; for from this sacred doctrine abstracts [5].

(1) *Ibid.,* art. 3, pp. 352-356.
(2) *Ibid.,* articles 3 to 11 inclusive, pp. 352-405.
(3) *Ibid ,* art. 12, pp. 406-407.
(4) *Ibid.,* art. 12, pp. 407-408.
(5) IOANN. a S. THOMA, *Cursus Theologicus,* Tome I, in Questionem I, Primae Partis, Disp. II, art. 1, p. 347 :
— ... Nomine enim doctrinae (ut dicitur I *Poster.* c. 1; et explicatur ibi a

For the meaning of *doctrina* the author has gone to Aristotle and St. Thomas. But it is difficult to see how he finds this meaning of doctrine in the text to which he refers. What Aristotle says is: *Omnis doctrina et omnis disciplina intellectiva ex praeexistenti fit cognitione.* And St. Thomas' commentary runs as follows:

> ... Primo, inducit universalem propositionem propositum continentem, scilicet quod acceptio cognitionis in nobis fit ex aliqua praeexistenti cognitione. Et ideo dicit: *Omnis doctrina et omnis disciplina,* non autem omnis cognitio, quia non omnis cognitio ex priori cognitione dependet: esset enim in infinitum abire. Nomen autem doctrinae et disciplinae ad cognitionis acquisitionem pertinet. Nam doctrina est actio eius, qui aliquid cognoscere facit; disciplina autem est receptio cognitionis ab alio. Non autem accipitur hic doctrina et disciplina secundum quod se habent ad acquisitionem scientiae tantum, sed ad acquisitionem cognitionis cuiuscumque (ed. Leon., Tome I, p. 140).

Actually we do not find either Aristotle or St. Thomas speaking of *doctrina* as *cognitio.* *Doctrina* is rather distinguished from knowledge in so far as it proceeds from knowledge. Moreover, St. Thomas says that the word *doctrina* names the action of one who causes something to be known; it is an action of a teacher. But nothing is said about this action being in the teacher. Rather, from the general principle used both by Aristotle and St. Thomas that *actio est in passo,* we would say that this action proceeding from the teacher is in the disciple, the patient. We shall have occasion to discuss this point in the second chapter.

However, as this is the only text which the author cites for his interpretation of the term *doctrina* as *cognitio probativa in docente,* we do not feel secure in following him through to his conclusion that sacred doctrine is *cognitio probativa ex revelatis,* the sense in which he understands the word to be used in the first article of the *Summa.*

Moreover, in interpreting the word *sacra doctrina* in this sense in the first article, the author runs into the same sort of difficulty as that encountered by Sylvius in explaining the necessity of sa-

D. Thoma, lect. 1) intelligitur quaecumque cognitio probativa; quae in docente nominatur doctrina, in addiscente vero disciplina. Unde ad rationem doctrinae requiritur id quod ad probativam cognitionem: scilicet aliquid per modum principii inferentis seu probantis, et aliquid per modum conclusionis illatae et probatae. Unde patet, quod nomine sacrae doctrinae intelligitur cognitio probativa ex revelatis; haec enim dicitur cognitio sacra; et ita quae per cognitionem revelatam probantur, nomine sacrae doctrinae intelliguntur, sive probatio fiat probabiliter, sive scientifice: ab hoc enim abstrahit.

cred doctrine. Sylvius had to explain how theology the science is necessary. John of St. Thomas must explain how theology as doctrine is necessary. Sylvius explained his difficulty away by saying that theology at least in one of its parts or in one of its participated forms is necessary. John of St. Thomas appears to face his difficulty more objectively. He admits that according to his interpretation St. Thomas must be regarded as proving the necessity of sacred doctrine only in a compendious and virtual manner. What St. Thomas actually proves is the necessity of knowing supernatural truth which is beyond the philosophical disciplines. Virtually, however, he proves the necessity of some proof or discourse regarding this supernatural truth, and hence the necessity of sacred doctrine or theology as doctrine [1].

I honestly do not understand how one can say that, when St. Thomas concludes his argument in article one, he has only virtually proved the necessity of *sacra doctrina*. Yet John of St. Thomas is forced to say this in order to maintain his interpretation of the term.

CHENU

Many have seen this difficulty under which John of St. Thomas was laboring. Father M.-D. Chenu, O.P., takes refuge in the ambiguity of the term in an age of theological development when terminology was lagging behind the development of ideas and doctrines [2].

The signification of the term *sacra doctrina* was gradually extended from its fundamental meaning in Lombard's time as an exegesis of Scripture making use of the resources of rhetoric [3] to

(1) IOANN. a S. THOMA, *Curs. Theol.*, Tome I, in Quaestionem I Primae Partis, Disp. II, art. 1, p. 348:
— ... Respondetur: D. Thomas compendio et virtualiter probasse necessitatem theologiae ut est doctrina, ostendendo necessitatem cognoscendi veritatem supernaturalem, quae non potest attingi per philosophicas disciplinas; nam hoc ipso quod nobis necessaria est aliqua veritas revelata, necessaria nobis est aliqua probatio et discursus circa illa: alias non posset declarari, nec defendi. Hoc ergo tamquam per se notum et facile reliquit D. Thomas, et solum probavit primum, in quo est difficultas, scilicet quod talis veritas revelata sit necessaria: inde enim probavit quod etiam virtualiter revelata erit necessaria seu utilis...
(2) M.-D. CHENU, O.P., *La théologie comme science au XIIIe siècle.*² Pro manuscripto. Paris: J. Vrin, 1943, pp. 125, cf. p. 86. (This work is a revised and enlarged edition of his article of the same title in *Archives d'Histoire doctrinale et littéraire du Moyen Age,* II (1927), pp. 31-71).
(3) *Ibid*, p. 34.

3

the indetermined signification of two things, namely, revelation itself and the intellectual effervescence which revelation causes in man [1]. And the word retains its technical equivocity even in the language of St. Thomas, who distinguishes at the interior of *sacra doctrina* the habit of faith from the habit of theology [2]. In the following two paragraphs Fr. Chenu summarizes his opinion for us : [3]

« Nous pouvons maintenant reconnaître le contenu et apprécier le sens du terme *sacra doctrina*, dont nous avons plusieurs fois déjà signalé l'indétermination dans la langue commune du temps, qui recouvre tout le champ de l'enseignement chrétien depuis l'équivalence avec la *sacra scriptura* jusqu'à la spéculation théologique, qui, dans la première question de la Somme de saint Thomas, embrasse les problèmes allant de la nécessité de la révélation jusqu'à la légitimité de l'argumentation rationnelle, qui par conséquent déborde le sens technique particulier donné aujourd'hui au mot *théologie* (2). *Sacra doctrina*, c'est l'enseignement procédant de la révélation : avec toutes les ressources qui en découlent, avec tous les traitements qu'elle peut comporter dans l'esprit humain, de la lecture de la Bible à la déduction théologique. Donc diversité relative d'objets, de fonctions, de méthodes. De tout ce que nous avons dit il ressort, que saint Thomas a distingué Écriture et théologie, foi et théologie (1) ; il a même, dès les Sentences, expressément affirmé la diversité de deux *habitus* (2). Mais la terminologie est in retard sur les idées et la doctrine, comme il arrive dans les sciences en progrès ; l'extension indéterminée de *doctrina sacra* demeure un vestige de l'état antérieur de la théologie où la diversification méthodologique n'était pas accomplie (cf. notre chap. I) (3).

Du moins ce terme unique porte-t-il aussi témoignage en faveur de la continuité organique qui, à travers les diverses fonctions et étapes du savoir sacré, en assure l'unité, dans la foi qui le commande, le dilate, le construit, et toujours anime. *Fides est quasi habitus theologiae* (4). Ce serait faute grave de « diviser » la théologie, sous prétexte d'en répartir les fonctions et les méthodes. Le vocable *doctrina sacra* n'est point périmé.

Although Fr. Chenu says that we cannot parcel out the various senses of the term *doctrina sacra* to particular articles in the first question of the *Summa*, he nevertheless speaks of three senses of the term : the general sense (revelation), the technical sense (science), and the Scriptural sense [4]. It is clear that in so far as he

(1) *Ibid.*, p. 39.
(2) *Ibid.*, pp. 39, 69.
(3) *Ibid*, pp. 85-86. We should note here that the quotation from St. Thomas in this paragraph, *fides est quasi habitus theologiae* (*in Boethii de Trin.*, q. 5, a. 4, ad 8), should read *fides ... est quasi habitus principiorum Theologiae* according to the autograph (Codex Vat. lat. 9850), published in part by Paul Wyser, O.P. (Fribourg-Louvain, 1948).
(4) *Ibid.*, p. 86, n. 1. Cf. also the first redaction of this work, p. 68.

permits the term to be used of revelation and Scripture his opinion differs from that of John of St. Thomas.

It is particularly worthy of note that according to Fr. Chenu's opinion articles 9 and 10 of the first question of the *Summa* do not logically belong to the treatise which Thomas is here exposing. These articles according to Fr. Chenu appear in the treatise only out of St. Thomas' deference to usage. The internal logic of his theory will eliminate them in the course of time.[1]

Father Chenu's work as an historian of medieval theology merits great respect, and hence his observations on the development and extension of the meaning of the term *sacra doctrina* in the 12th and 13th centuries must be duly considered. Whether or not he has sufficiently probed the text of St. Thomas in regard to the meaning of this term can be determined only after a positive examination of St. Thomas' use of the term.

Fr. M.-R. Gagnebet, O.P., has not treated the question of the signification of the term *sacra doctrina* with the same detail as Fr. Chenu. His opinion, so far as he expresses it, is similar to that of Fr. Chenu [2].

Fr. R. Garrigou-Lagrange, O.P., says that the opinion of John of St. Thomas and Sylvius seems to be the true one in the controversy over the meaning of this term [3] and Monsignor M. Grabmann is inclined to follow the lead of Fr. Garrigou-Lagrange [4]. Let us read what Fr. Garrigou-Lagrange has to say [5]:

Quoad definitionem nominalem, seu quoad sensum huiusce expressionis « *sacra doctrina* » est controversia. Quid per haec verba intelligat sanctus Doctor: an fidem? an theologiam? an doctrinam sacram in communi prout abstrahit a

---

(1) M.-D. CHENU, O.P., « La théologie comme science... », *Archives d'Hist. doct. et litt. du Moyen Age*, II (1927), pp. 31-71, - p. 69:
— Là encore, l'explication nous paraît facile; puisqu'il était reçu, à l'entrée de la doctrine sacrée, de traiter des sens de l'Écriture, saint Thomas se conforme à l'usage, que pourtant, bientôt, la logique interne de sa théorie éliminera. On observera d'ailleurs que déjà cet exposé d'herméneutique sacrée n'est plus, comme dans le Commentaire des Sentences (q. 1, a. 5), bloqué en un seul article avec l'exposé de la méthode théologique. Le temps fera le reste.
(2) M.-R. GAGNEBET, O.P., *La nature de la théologie spéculative*, Revue Thomiste, XLIV (1938), pp. 1-39, 213-255, 645-674; - cf. pp. 219-220, n. 1.
(3) R. GARRIGOU-LAGRANGE, O.P., *De Deo Uno. Commentarium in Primam Partem S. Thomae*. Paris: Desclée de Brouwer et Cie., 1938, pp. 582, - p. 36.
(4) M. GRABMANN, *Die theologische Erkenntnis - und Einleitungslehre des heiligen Thomas von Aquin auf Grund seiner Schrift in Boethium de Trinitate*. (Thomistische Studien: IV. Band). Freiburg in der Schweiz: Paulusverlag, 1948, pp. XV - 392, - p. 125.
(5) *Op. cit.*, p. 36.

fide et a theologia. Caietanus et plures alii hoc ultimum tenent; sed Ioannes a Sancto Thoma, Sylvius et alii contendunt sanctum Thomam hic intelligere theologiam proprie dictam. Haec secunda responsio videtur vera, quamvis enim in art. 1⁰ agatur potius de sacra doctrina in communi; ab articulo 2⁰ iam est sermo proprie de scientia sacra prout distinguitur a fide. Paulatim sanctus Thomas transit a notione confusa ad distinctam.

I find the paragraph confusing. First of all, Sylvius and John of St. Thomas are not of the same opinion in this matter, as we have seen [1]. Moreover, the first meaning of the term *sacra doctrina* as given by John of St. Thomas is not *theologia proprie dicta* [2]. And finally, we get the impression from this paragraph that the interpretation of *sacra doctrina* as *theologia proprie dicta* is regarded as the true interpretation, whereas Fr. Garrigou-Lagrange's own interpretation, as indicated in his comments on the first and second article, is rather a compromise between the interpretations of Cajetan and John of St. Thomas [3].

Thus Fr. Garrigou-Lagrange understands the term *sacra doctrina* in the first article of the *Summa* in three different senses: first, as revealed knowledge abstracting from faith and theology (the opinion of Cajetan); secondly, as faith, in so far as faith and not theology is necessary for salvation (this sense of *sacra doctrina* seems to be original with Fr. Garrigou-Lagrange); and thirdly, as theology, the science of sacred theology. He understands the term in the second article to mean the science of sacred theology. He does not discuss the relation of the term *sacra doctrina* to Sacred Scripture.

As Fr. Garrigou-Lagrange gives no explicit reasons for his in-

(1) Cf. above, pp. 23, 27-28. Fr. Billuart, who follows Sylvius' opinion, makes the following statement which seems to inspire that of Fr. Garrigou-Lagrange: « Ioannes a S. Thoma, Sylvius et plures alii e contra contendunt S. Thomam per sacram doctrinam in hoc primo articulo intelligere theologiam proprie sumptam;... » (*Summa Sancti Thomae Hodiernis Academiarum Moribus Accommodata*. Parisiis-Lugduni: Lecoffre, 1878, Tomus I. Dissertatio Prooemialis, art. 2, p. 4).
(2) Cf. above, pp. 27-29.
(3) *Op. cit.*, pp. 38-39: — In corpore primi articuli nondum agitur de scientia theologica, sed de doctrina sacra prout abstrahit a fide et a theologia, et etiam est sermo de fide, prout fides et non theologia est ad salutem necessaria...
In responsione, *ad Qum*, iam est sermo de theologia prout distinguitur a fide,... (p. 38).
.....
St. Quaestionis: Ex hoc titulo [art. 2] apparet quod agitur nunc non solum de sacra doctrina in communi prout abstrahit a fide et a theologia, sed de scientia theologica (p. 39).

terpretation of the term, his opinion can be evaluated only later in the light of our positive investigation.

Fr. J. Rimaud is of the opinion that the term *sacra doctrina* as used in the first article of the *Summa* means dogma, and in the second article means the science of dogma or theology in the modern sense of the word [1].

BONNEFOY

The interpretation which Fr. Bonnefoy gives to the term *sacra doctrina* is entirely different from that of any of his predecessors. His study is the most extended treatment of the question that has been written in modern times, and so deserves to be considered in some detail [2].

Fr. Bonnefoy's study follows the plan he sets down for himself in the early part of his work. He will first determine the relation between *sacra doctrina* and *Sacra Scriptura* by means of a comparative analysis of the pertinent articles of the *Commentary on the Sentences* and the *Summa*. Having determined that these terms are equivalent in their signification and accepting the common interpretation of theologians that the terms *sacra doctrina* and *theologia* are equivalent, he will procede to show what *Sacra Scriptura* and *theologia* have in common and to what extent they are identical with *sacra doctina* [3].

Like Cajetan and Sylvius, Fr. Bonnefoy rejects *a priori* the equivocity of the term *sacra doctrina*. But unlike Cajetan and Sylvius,

(1) J. RIMAUD., *Thomisme et Méthode*. Paris, Beauchesne, 1925, p. 65, n. 1.

(2) J. FR. BONNEFOY, O.F.M., *La nature de la théologie selon saint Thomas d'Aquin*, Paris: J. Vrin - Bruges: Ch. Beyaert, 1939, pp. 88. Previously printed as: « La théologie comme science et l'explication de la foi selon S. Thomas d'Aquin », *Ephemerides Theologicae Lovanienses*, XIV (1937), pp. 421-446; 600-631; XV (1938), pp. 491-516. Cf. also Fr. Bonnefoy's article, « La méthodologie théologique de saint Thomas », *Revista Española de Teología*, X (1950), pp. 41-81.

(3) J. FR. BONNEFOY, O.F.M., *La nature de la Théologie...*, p. 11: — Ce terme de sacra doctrina a donc une certaine équivalence et avec le terme de théologie et avec celui d'Écriture. La première n'est pas contestée et ressort avec évidence du fait que saint Thomas traite de cette *doctrina sacra* pour délimiter l'objet de sa *Somme Théologique*. Nous ne nous attarderons pas à la prouver. — La seconde est communément rejetée par ses interprètes: nous l'établirons par une analyse comparée des articles du *Commentaire* et de la *Somme*. Cette double équivalence étant acquise, nous aurons à établir ce qu'ont de commun, selon saint Thomas, l'Écriture Sainte et la théologie, et jusqu'à quel point s'applique le principe: *Quae sunt eadem uni tertio, sunt eadem inter se.*

Fr. Bonnefoy does not rest content with *a priori* reasonings; his *a priori* reasoning is always examined *a posteriori* by a detailed analysis of the text[1].

The point of departure of the whole investigation made by Fr. Bonnefoy is the definition of *sacra doctrina* which he finds delineated in the first article of the *Commentary on the Sentences* and defined with completeness by St. Thomas himself in the first article of the *Summa*.

> Les vérités révélées par Dieu, s'imposent comme telles à notre foi: nous aurions pu le déduire et donner, de la doctrine sacrée, une définition complète. Saint Thomas l'a fait lui-même: *sunt tamen a Deo revelata suscipienda per fidem... et in huiusmodi sacra doctrina constitit.* La doctrine sacrée est constituée par l'ensemble des vérités que Dieu nous a révélées et que nous devons croire. (p. 13).

This definition, says Fr. Bonnefoy, corresponds to St. Thomas' first conception of *sacra doctrina*, found in the *Commentary*. With this definition St. Thomas marks off clearly that body of truth which is known by way of revelation in opposition to those bodies of truth which are discovered by unaided human reason. Moreover, within the body of truth known by way of revelation there is no distinction made between the truths of faith and theological conclusions, between the formally revealed and the virtually revealed. St. Thomas does not even insinuate such a distinction[2].

The opposition set up between *sacra doctrina* and the philosophical disciplines is affirmed in the *Sed Contra* and in the body of the article, and it appears again in the *ad secundum*, where St. Thomas opposes the light of natural reason and the light of divine revelation. And this opposition is always the same: not between natural truths and theology, as we currently understand theology; but between natural truths and the truths of faith, theology in the sense of truths formally revealed. This acceptation of the term « theology » will not be disconcerting to the historian of medieval

(1) *Ibid.*, pp. 9-10
(2) *Ibid.*, p. 13 : — Saint Thomas a donc maintenu dans la *Somme* sa première conception de la *sacra doctrina* et, pas plus que dans le *Commentaire*, il n'a insinué de distinction à faire entre les vérités de foi et les conclusions théologiques, entre le formellement révélé et le virtuellement révélé. Ayant démontré la nécessité d'une doctrine révélée s'opposant aux disciplines philosophiques et les complétant, il la nomme *doctrina sacra,* la définit et aborde incontinent les questions suivantes : *Utrum sacra doctrina sit scientia. Utrum... sit una ?*

doctrine. Like the term *sacra doctrina,* the term theology in this sense was used ordinarily to designate Sacred Scripture itself. We find St. Thomas doing it himself: *et haec est theologia, quae sacra Scriptura dicitur (in Boethii de Trin.,* q. 5, a. 4)[1].

With the definition of *sacra doctrina* found in this first article of the *Summa* and with a preliminary indication of a certain equivalence between this term and the terms *theologia* and *Sacra Scriptura* in the sense that one can be substituted or understood for another, Fr. Bonnefoy proceeds to show that what is virtually contained here in this first article is methodically unfolded in the course of the remaining articles of the question. And the answer to the important question whether *sacra doctrina* can claim the name of science on the same score as the philosophical disciplines is already found here in germ[2].

Father Bonnefoy then takes up each of the following nine articles of the first question with parallel passages from the *Commentary* and proceeds to show how this definition of sacred doctrine is either supposed or verified and the equivalence of *sacra doctrina* with *Sacra Scriptura.*

In article 10 Fr. Bonnefoy finds the clue which will enable him to distinguish *sacra doctrina* from *Sacra Scriptura,* — to show what they have in common and how they are distinct. For here a subtle change is discovered in St. Thomas' manner of speaking. He speaks no longer of *sacra doctrina,* but of *Scriptura Sacra huius doctrinae.*

---

(1) *Ibid.,* p. 14 : — En opposant la lumière de la raison naturelle et la lumière de la révélation divine *(ad* 2) saint Thomas continue donc à opposer aux vérités naturelles, non ce que nous entendons par théologie, mais les vérités de foi, les vérités formellement révélées. Cette acception du terme « théologie » n'a rien qui puisse déconcerter l'historien des doctrines médiévales. Tout comme le terme *doctrina sacra,* il s'employait couramment pour désigner l'Écriture Sainte elle même.
The text which Fr. Bonnefoy proceeds to cite from Thomas' *Com. in Boethii de Trinitate* includes the expression *theologia, quae sacra Scriptura dicitur.* This reading, hower, is defective. It should read *theologia, quae in sacra Scriptura traditur.* Cf. the autograph *Cod. vat. lat.* 9850 (ed. Wyser, p. 48).

(2) *Ibid.,* p. 15 : — On ne peut établir l'existence d'un être, sans le faire connaître au moins confusément. Saint Thomas a donc été amené, par la force des choses, à donner une première esquisse de la doctrine sacrée. L'article 1er contient virtuellement ce que les autres exposeront avec méthode. Le Docteur Angélique y a défini le contenu de la doctrine sacrée: *a Deo revelata suscipienda per fidem,* et l'a opposée aux doctrines philosophiques *quae sunt secundum rationem humanam inventae.* Cette doctrine sacrée, peut-elle au même titre que ces disciplines revendiquer la titre de science ? - *Respondeo dicendum sacram doctrinam esse scientiam* (art. 2).

« *Cet article 10 devait, puisqu'il se rapportait aux signes, distinguer la doctrine sacrée et l'Écriture Sainte. Les neuf précédents, au contraire, envisageaient les choses signifiées et pouvaient identifier la doctrine de l'Écriture exposée par les hommes ou doctrine sacrée avec l'Écriture elle-même* » (p. 27).

It is in the light of this discovery that Fr. Bonnefoy compares *Sacra Scriptura* with « la doctrine sacrée ou théologie ». He has not stopped to prove the equivalence of *sacra doctrina* and *theologia*; he has merely noted indications of it along the way, because this equivalence, he says, is generally admitted.

Scripture differs from doctrine on two counts; there is a difference in the order of exposition and a difference in language. Scripture and sacred doctrine are identical, however, by reason of their origin, their certitude, their object, and their content.

Si maintenant nous comparons un tel exposé avec l'Écriture, nous constatons des différences. La disposition matérielle n'est plus la même; un ordre logique a remplacé l'ordre chronologique prédominant dans la Bible. Par le fait même, l'argumentation assez peu employée dans l'Écriture, occupe dans cette transposition la première place[1]. Le langage enfin n'est plus le même: ce n'est plus la parole de Dieu, mais la parole des hommes redisant à leur façon les pensées divines. On ne peut donc pas appliquer aux ouvrages des saints Pères et des autres commentateurs de l'Écriture les règles d'herméneutique propres à la Bible. Et c'est pourquoi saint Thomas, quand il en vient aux règles d'interprétation, ne parle plus de *doctrina sacra*, mais de *Scriptura sacra huius doctrinae* ou de *Scriptura sacra* tout court.

. . . . .

Identiques, la doctrine sacrée ou théologie et l'Écriture sainte le sont par leur origine et, partant, par leur certitude...

Identiques, la doctrine sacrée et l'Écriture le seront encore par leur objet et leur contenu... (p. 27).

Thus in his conclusion Fr. Bonnefoy has prepared the way for the problems to be discussed in the next two chapters: II – *La doctrine sacrée comme science*; and III – *L'explication de la foi*. And the solutions to be given to these problems are already clearly foreshadowed.

La transposition en un language technique et la mise en ordre des vérités doctrinales contenues dans l'Écriture ne les empêchent pas de demeurer ce qu'elles sont originellement: un commentaire, une explication des principales vérités de foi énoncées dans le Symbole... La doctrine sacrée sera science dans la mesure où l'Écriture elle-même l'est... (p. 28).

40

This rather long exposition of Fr. Bonnefoy's procedure was necessary in order for us to know just where to begin to examine the accuracy of his work. The reviews which have been published regarding his work, whether favorable or unfavorable, have failed to touch the critical point in the exposition of his thesis. This critical point reduces itself to the definition of *sacra doctrina* which he finds in the first article. For if this definition *certainly* represents what St. Thomas meant by *sacra doctrina*, the main conclusions of Fr. Bonnefoy's thesis would necessarily follow, and supposing St. Thomas to be consistent with himself, the interpretations given to texts which he uses to confirm *a posteriori* this definition should be accepted. If, however, this definition does not represent what St. Thomas means by *sacra doctrina*, then the whole problem of the identification of *sacra doctrina* with *Scriptura Sacra* will have to be re-examined and reworked. This would also bring into question the conclusions which follow from this identification as well as the exegesis of texts wherein the *a posteriori* confirmation of these conclusions has been found.

The role which this definition plays in Fr. Bonnefoy's study should not, however, be misunderstood. He does not use it as a principle of demonstration, except when he wishes to indicate *a priori* the conclusion which he will establish *a posteriori* from a detailed examination of the text. But although it is not used as a positive principle, it nevertheless serves as a purely negative norm for the interpretation of many, if not all, of the texts he examines. And this procedure is not to be quarrelled with, if it is true that St. Thomas has actually given a definition of *sacra doctrina* in the first article.

Let us then examine the text of the first article where Fr. Bonnefoy finds St. Thomas defining *sacra doctrina*. Fr. Bonnefoy does not cite the complete text himself, so we will do it here. As it is a response to an objection, the objection also must be cited:

1. Ad ea enim quae supra rationem sunt, homo non debet conari, secundum illud *Eccli.* III, 22: « Altiora te ne quaesieris ». Sed ea quae rationi subduntur, sufficienter traduntur in philosophicis disciplinis. Superfluum igitur videtur praeter philosophicas disciplinas aliam doctrinam haberi.

. . . . .

Ad primum ergo. Dicendum quod licet ea quae sunt altiora hominis cognitione, non sint ab homine per rationem inquirenda, sunt tamen a Deo revelata, suscipienda per fidem. Unde et ibidem subditur: « Plurima supra sensum hominum ostensa sunt tibi ». Et in huiusmodi sacra doctrina consistit. (*S. T.*, I, 1, 1, ad 1m).

The words cited by Fr. Bonnefoy as giving the definition of *sacra doctrina* are the following: *sunt tamen a Deo revelata suscipienda per fidem ... et in huiusmodi sacra doctrina constitit.* And Fr. Bonnefoy rephrases the sentence thus: *La doctrine sacrée est constituée par l'ensemble des vérités que Dieu nous a révélées et que nous devons croire* (p. 13) [1].

The first thing to notice is what the phrase *a Deo revelata suscipienda per fidem* refers to. The reference is clear: namely, *altiora hominis cognitione*. Moreover, this phrase is again clarified by the corresponding phrase in the objection: *ea quae supra rationem sunt*. In the body of the article St. Thomas has proved the necessity of *sacra doctrina* if man is to have knowledge of this kind of truth, a knowledge which is necessary for salvation; reason cannot give this knowledge hence *sacra doctrina* is necessary. Now in this response St. Thomas says: Granted that man should not try to investigate this kind of truth by reason, these truths are nevertheless revealed by God and to be accepted through faith. He is not referring to the kind of truth which can be known by reason, *ea quae rationi subduntur*. He omits consideration of this aspect of the objection for two reasons: first, he will consider it in the next response; secondly, the answer to the first objection does not require that it be considered. So the things which are revealed by God and are to be accepted by faith are those truths which are above human reason by reason of the fact that *in themselves* they are impervious to reason. We would call these truths mysteries, and, of course, they are to be accepted through faith: *sunt tamen a Deo revelata, suscipienda per fidem*. This is the only possible way for man to know these truths with certainty.

The text continues: *... et in huiusmodi sacra doctrina constitit*. In this phrase the reading of the text comes into question. The text as quoted by Fr. Bonnefoy employs the word *constitit*. Most probably this reading is simply a printing mistake made by the publishers. For this reading does not occur in any of the standard editions of the *Summa*: for example, it is not in the Piana edition (also known as the first Roman edition, or *editio Vaticana*), nor in the Vives edition, nor in the Parma and Leonine editions; moreover, it is not referred to as a variant reading in the Leonine

---

(1) This « definition » either in the words of St. Thomas or in the paraphrase of Fr. Bonnefoy appears again on pages 15, 27, 28, 45, 48, 70.

edition. There are variant readings of the phrase *in huiusmodi*; in the *Codex Vatic.* 4330, for example, we find the reading *ex his* and in several other codices we read *in his*. The Leonine editors prefer the reading *in huiusmodi*.

However, the variant readings do not alter, in so far as we can judge, the substantial meaning of the text; even the reading of *constitit* for *consistit* does not alter the sense.

Fr. Bonnefoy paraphrases these words as follows: « *La doctrine sacrée est constituée* ... ». And the meaning of his expression *est constituée* can be judged from his restatement of the definition at the beginning of chapter two: « La doctrine sacrée étant l'ensemble des vérités immédiatement révélées par Dieu et imposées à notre foi ... » (p. 28).

Hence he understands *sacra doctrina* to consist in truths revealed by God in the sense that the body of these revealed truths is identical with *sacra doctrina*.

St. Thomas, however, uses the expression *consistere in* in many different ways. We find this expression modified by various adverbs which serve to make precise the sense intended. For example, *consistere in* is modified by *originaliter et substantialiter* and *formaliter et completive* [1], *principaliter* and *secundario* [2], *radicaliter* and *significative* [3], *essentialiter* [4], *totaliter* [5].

The exact sense in which the term is used is not always expressed. For example, in one text St. Thomas will say that beatitude consists in the fruition of God [6], and in another text that beatitude consists in the vision of God [7]. Now since fruition is an act of the will and vision is an act of the intellect, it is evident that the expression *consistere in* in these texts must be understood in the light of what St. Thomas elsewhere says about beatitude.

Likewise in regard to *sacra doctrina*, when St. Thomas says that it consists in truths revealed by God which are in themselves above human reason and which are to be accepted on faith, we must interpret the expression *consists in* in the light of the context and in the light of what St. Thomas elsewhere says about *sacra*

---

(1) *Quaest. Quodl.*, qd. 8, q. 9, a. 1 (19).
(2) *S. T.* II-II, 84, 2, ad 2.
(3) *S. T.* II-II, 145, 1, ad 3.
(4) *S. T.* II-II, 26, 2c.
(5) *S. T.* II-II, 188, 6c.
(6) *S. T.* III, 7, 4, ad 2.
(7) *S. T.* I-II, 4, 5c.

doctrina. Now he tells us frequently that this sort of truth serves as the principles of sacred doctrine. Hence sacred doctrine must be said to consist in this sort of truth as in its principles, i. e. *originaliter* or *radicaliter* or *principaliter*. This meaning of the expression *consistere in* is altogether different from the meaning which Fr. Bonnefoy gives to the expression.

Moreover, if it be true, according to our analysis of this response, that the kind of truth referred to here is that which is in itself beyond human reason, then according to Fr. Bonnefoy *sacra doctrina* should include only those truths which we would call mysteries. However, Fr. Bonnefoy does not and would not say this sort of thing, for the reason that he does not understand the phrase *a Deo revelata suscipienda per fidem* as referring only to truths which are in themselves beyond reason, as the text demands.

He understands the phrase *a Deo revelata suscipienda per fidem* to refer not only to truths which in themselves are above human reason but also to natural truths which God has revealed. He seems not only to have lost sight of the context of the objection but to have failed to keep clearly in mind the twofold opposition which Thomas sets up in this first article.

In the body of the article and in the first objection and response, St. Thomas clearly opposes two kinds of truths: one which is in itself beyond human reason, the other which is within the power of unaided reason. In the body of the article St. Thomas shows the necessity of *sacra doctrina* in regard to both kinds of truth. This is the first opposition – between truths which are in themselves beyond human reason and truths which are within the power of reason.

The second opposition is not between the truths considered in themselves, but between modes of knowledge. Thus *sacra doctrina* and the philosophical disciplines are opposed because they are diverse modes of knowledge. The fact that *sacra doctrina* provides man with a knowledge of truths which in themselves are beyond his reason but which are necessary for his salvation proves the necessity of *sacra doctrina*. However, to prove the adequate distinction of *sacra doctrina* from the *philosophical disciplines* this is not enough, for doctrines and sciences are not distinguished by truths considered in themselves; diverse sciences can demonstrate the same truths. Hence St. Thomas brings out clearly in the second response that it is the *formalis ratio cognoscibilis* that induces diversity among sciences. And thus a second opposition appears in the first article, namely between modes of knowledge and not merely between truths considered in themselves.

Fr. Bonnefoy confuses these two oppositions in the first article. St. Thomas does not say that every truth which *sacra doctrina* considers is to be accepted on faith; but those truths which *in themselves* are beyond human reason and which are revealed by God are to be accepted on faith. Then in the 2nd response St. Thomas shows that even in regard to those truths which in themselves are not above reason, the mode of knowledge in which *sacra doctrina* regards these truths is diverse from the mode of knowledge in which the philosophical disciplines regard these truths. In regard to these truths St. Thomas does not say that they are to be accepted on faith in *sacra doctrina,* but that *sacra doctrina* considers them in so far as they are knowable by the light of divine revelation, whereas the philosophical disciplines consider them in so far as they are knowable by the light of natural reason. The opposition in question here is one of modes of knowledge.

Now although the truth that the earth is round which both astrologer and natural philosopher demonstrate, is materially and considered in itself the same truth, nevertheless this truth *as known* by the astrologer through his principles and *as known* by the natural philosopher through his principles is formally diverse. And hence one can say that this truth as known by the astrologer is beyond the power of the natural philosopher who is limited to his own principles.

Likewise - although the truth that God is one, which both metaphysics and sacred doctrine consider, is the same truth considered in itself, nevertheless as known by the metaphysician through his principles and as known through the principles of sacred doctrine, this truth is formally diverse. And hence one can say that this truth in so far as it is the object of sacred doctrine is beyond the power of the metaphysician who is limited to his own principles.

But it is one thing to say that a truth *in itself* is beyond the power of a science or beyond the power of human reason and quite a different thing to say that a truth as known through the principles of a higher mode of knowledge is beyond the power of the principles of a lower mode of knowledge.

Hence, too, it is one thing to say that revealed truths which in themselves are above the power of unaided reason must be accepted in an act of faith, and quite another thing to say that revealed truths which are not in themselves above the power of unaided reason but in so far as they are the object of sacred doctrine must be accepted in an act of faith. St. Thomas has made the first statement in the response under discussion. He has not made the second statement.

Fr. Bonnefoy, however, thinks that he has. And his interpretation seems to be due in great part to his failure to keep clearly in mind the twofold opposition which St. Thomas speaks of in his first article, the first of which is between truths in themselves beyond the power of unaided reason and truths in themselves within the power of unaided reason, and the second being between the modes of knowledge in which these truths are known.

The confusion of this twofold opposition is particularly noticeable in the following paragraph from Fr. Bonnefoy's study [1]:

> La distinction entre *revelata* et *revelabilia* n'oppose donc pas le formellement révélé au virtuellement révélé, comme l'assurent maints commentateurs de la *Somme*[1], mais deux groupes de vérités formellement révélées, déjà distinguées dans l'article 1er de la *Somme:* celles *quae rationem humanam excedunt* et celles *quae de Deo ratione humana investigari possunt.* Ce second groupe de vérités, révélées de fait, mais connaissables ou même connues par la raison naturelle, pouvait paraître faire échec à l'unité de la doctrine sacrée définie « l'ensemble des vérités révélées par Dieu et imposées à notre foi ». A cette objection, saint Thomas répond: ce n'est pas en tant que connaissables par la raison naturelle, mais en tant que connaissables et connues par la révélation — *revelabilia* — que ces vérités appartiennent à la doctrine sacrée. Elles ont donc même raison formelle que les vérités qui dépassent la raison humain: *omnia quaecumque sunt divinitus revelabilia communicant in una ratione formali obiecti huius scientiae* (art. 3, *in corp*).

Fr. Bonnefoy has here identified « l'ensemble des vérités révélées par Dieu et imposées à notre foi » (which in the text refers to revealed truths which *in themselves* are above the power of unaided reason) with revealed truths in so far as they are the object of *doctrina sacra*.

Hence in this one text where Fr. Bonnefoy finds the definition of *sacra doctrina* it appears that there are two points which he has not sufficiently considered: 1) the meaning of the expression *consistere in*, and 2) what truths are referred to in the phrase *a Deo revelata suscipienda per fidem*.

(1) *Op. cit.*, pp. 18-19.

Of course, this is not the only text Fr. Bonnefoy appeals to for his definition of *doctrina sacra*. He opens his discussion of the definition of this term with a consideration of the text in the *Commentary* where we find the doublet of the first article of the *Summa*. In this text he finds the first delineation of the complete definition of *sacra doctrina* found in the *Summa*. Let us cite this text and its interpretation in Fr. Bonnefoy's study [1].

Ad huius evidentiam sciendum est, quod omnes qui recte senserunt posuerunt finem humanae vitae, Dei contemplationem. Contemplatio autem Dei est duplex. Una per creaturas, quae imperfecta est... in qua contemplatione Philosophus, X *Ethic.*, cap. IX, felicitatem contemplativam posuit, quae tamen est felicitas viae; et ad hanc ordinatur tota cognitio philosophica, quae ex rationibus creaturarum procedit. Est alia Dei contemplatio, qua videtur immediate per suam essentiam: Et haec perfecta est quae erit in patria et est homini possibilis secundum *fidei suppositionem*. Unde oportet ut ea quae sunt ad finem proportionentur fini, quatenus homo manuducatur ad illam contemplationem in statu viae per cognitionem non a creaturis sumptam, sed *immediate ex divino umine [lumine] inspiratam;* et haec est doctrina theologiae[1] ».

La doctrine sacrée, ou *doctrina theologiae,* consiste donc dans les vérités immédiatement révélées par Dieu et, comme telles, imposées à notre foi. Elle s'oppose aux disciplines philosophiques qui s'acquièrent par l'exercice de la raison naturelle.

Après cette première distinction entre vérités naturelles et vérités de foi, saint Thomas aurait du, pour arriver à notre conception de la théologie, distinguer entre vérité explicitement et implicitement révélées; ou rappeler l'adage de saint Augustin, si opportunément inscrit par saint Bonaventure au frontispice de ses deux oeuvres de théologie générale: *quod intellegimus, debemus rationi; quod credimus, auctoritati*[2]. Rien de semblable dans le *Commentaire*. Ayant opposé aux doctrines philosophiques la doctrine immédiatement révélée, il conclut à la nécessité de la théologie: *et haec est doctrina theologiae,* et passe outre. L'article suivant, loin d'insinuer une distinction entre vérités révélées et théologie affirmera l'unité de cette doctrine sacrée qu'il vient de présenter comme *cognitionem non a creaturis sumptam, sed immediate ex divino lumine inspiratam.*

To go right to the heart of the matter, Fr. Bonnefoy's conclusion from this text depends entirely on the reference assigned to the word *haec* in the phrase *et haec est doctrina theologiae*. If this word refers to *cognitionem... immediate ex divino lumine inspiratam,* as Fr. Bonnefoy's interpretation demands, then we would have some reason for agreeing with his conclusion that « La doctrine sacrée, ou *doctrina theologiae,* consiste donc dans les vérités immédiate-

(1) *Op. cit.,* p. 12.

ment révélées par Dieu et, comme telles, imposées à notre foi ». For *cognitio immediate ex divino lumine inspirata* signifies here quite clearly a knowledge which is faith. Hence *doctrina theologiae* in the phrase *et haec est doctrina theologiae* would thus be predicated of a knowledge which is faith, and thus could be said to consist in the truth immediately revealed by God and imposed on our faith.

Grammatically much can be said for this interpretation. However, a more thorough analysis of the text makes us begin to doubt about what the word *haec* refers to.

The division of the text may be visualized as follows:

> *Contemplatio* autem Dei est duplex:
> UNA per creaturas, quae imperfecta est...
> ALIA Dei contemplatio, qua videtur immediate per essentiam perfecta est quae erit in patria;
> et *haec* et homini possibilis (est) secundum suppositionem fidei.
> Unde oportet ut ea quae sunt ad finem proportionentur fini, quatenus homo manuducatur ad illam contemplationem in statu viae per cognitionem non a creaturis sumptam, sed immediate ex divino lumine inspiratam;
> et *haec* est doctrina theologiae.

Thus we see that the word which is being distinguished is *contemplatio: una, alia; et haec perfecta... in patria; et in statu viae (fini proportionata) ... haec est doctrina theologiae.* Thus *haec* can refer to that propaedeutic here on earth which is proportioned to the perfect contemplation which we will have in heaven, – *quatenus homo manuducatur ad illam contemplationem in statu viae per cognitionem... immediate ex divino lumine inspiratam.* Thus *haec* would refer not to *cognitionem... immediate ex lumine inspiratam,* but to that form of contemplation which can be described as *manuductio per cognitionem immediate ex divino lumine inspiratam in illam contemplationem quae perfecta erit in patria.* Thus later on in the same question of the prologue to the *Commentary,* after distinguishing clearly the habit of faith from the habit acquired in this doctrine [1], we find St. Thomas returning to almost the same formula of words to describe the sapiential character of this doctrine [2]:

> ... Sed tamen ratio manuducta per fidem excrescit in hoc ut ipsa credibilia plenius comprehendat, et tunc ipsa quodammodo intelligit: ...

(1) *In I Sent.*, prol., q. 1, a. 3, qa. 2, sol. 2, ad aliud (2m).
(2) *Ibid.*, a. 3, sol. 3.

The best we can say for Fr. Bonnefoy's interpretation is that it is grammatically sound (not that the other is not), and that it is a possible interpretation, if only this immediate context is taken into consideration. That his interpretation is the only correct one is certainly open to discussion.

Thus Fr. Bonnefoy's study of the first article of the *Summa* and its doublet in the *Commentary* in so far as it purports to result with certainty in a definition of *sacra doctrina* appears to lack the solidity of truly scholarly endeavor. Thus he has failed to determine the signification of *sacra doctrina* in the first article of the *Summa* and in its doublet in the *Commentary*.

The complete evaluation of Fr. Bonnefoy's work will emerge from the positive consideration of the text of St. Thomas which will occupy the third and fourth chapters of this study. Here we must be content with having indicated his procedure and pointed out the main deficiencies in his consideration of the first article of the *Summa*. These defects can be reduced to three: 1) he has erroneously considered the phrase *a Deo revelata suscipienda per fidem* to refer to all truths revealed by God, both truths which are in themselves within the power of reason and truths in themselves beyond reason; 2) he has not sufficiently considered the meaning of the phrase *in huiusmodi consistit* in the same response; and 3) his interpretation of the phrase *et haec est doctrina theologiae* is open to question.

CONGAR

Fr. M.-J. Congar, O.P., like Cajetan, Sylvius, and Bonnefoy, is convinced that the term *sacra doctrina* has the same sense from beginning to end of the first question of the *Summa*. He believes that Fr. Bonnefoy, however, has tampered with the thought of St. Thomas in identifying *sacra doctrina* with the body of truths immediately revealed by God and imposed on our faith. For this involves the consequence, as Fr. Bonnefoy himself declares, that the conclusions as well as the principles of this doctrine be accepted on faith. According to Father Congar, the expression *sacra doctrina* has a broader and more supple sense than that given by Fr. Bonnefoy [1].

(1) M.-J. CONGAR, O.P. [Comptes-Rendus], *Bulletin Thomiste,* V (1938-1939), pp. 490-505, - p. 500.

The meaning assigned to *sacra doctrina* by Fr. Congar is « enseignement révélé, *doctrina secundum revelationem divinam*, dans toute son ampleur » [1], « enseignement procédant de la Révélation » [2]. Thus the term *sacra doctrina* would embrace Sacred Scripture, catechesis, and preaching, as well as theology properly so called in its scientific form. These are but various parts or functions which can be distinguished at the interior of sacred doctrine [3].

In the second article where St. Thomas asks whether sacred doctrine is science, there is no question of strictly identifying sacred doctrine with science. There is question of knowing whether this Christian instruction, at least in one of its functions, in one of its acts, can verify the quality of science and merit the name of science. And St. Thomas answers that this Christian instruction verifies the quality of science according to the category of sciences defined by Aristotle as subalternated sciences [4].

Thus at the interior of this instruction various parts, various functions and acts can be distinguished. And the term *sacra doctrina* signifies this instruction in all its amplitude.

I would like to quote a paragraph in which Fr. Congar summarizes his account of the meaning of *sacra doctrina* [5].

Une étude du vocabulaire de la première question de la *Somme* (1) montre à l'évidence que la *sacra doctrina* dépasse la théologie au sens strict et englobe

(1) M.-J CONGAR, O.P., « Théologie », *Dictionnaire de Théologie Catholique*, XV, 1, cc. 341-502, - c. 379.
(2) M.-J. CONGAR., O.P., *Bulletin Thomiste* V (1938-1939), p. 500.
(3) M.-J. CONGAR, O.P., *Bulletin Thomiste* V (1938-1939) p. 500. Cf. also *DTC* XV, 1, c. 379 : ... — La *sacra doctrina* est l'enseignement révélé, *doctrina secundum revelationem divinam*, a. 1, dans toute son ampleur, dont l'objet est *ea quae ad christianam religionem pertinent*, prol.; elle s'oppose aux *philosophicae* (ou *physicae*) *disciplinae*, a. 1 et *Cont. Gent.*, 1. II, c. IV; elle comprend aussi bien l'Écriture Sainte, *Scriptura sacra huius doctrinae*, dit le prologue de la q. 1, la catéchèse et la prédication chrétienne, que la théologie proprement dite en sa forme scientifique.
(4) *DTC* XV, 1, c. 379 : — Nous soupçonnons dès lors ce que signifie l'a. 2, *Utrum sacra doctrina sit scientia ?* En posant cette question, saint Thomas prend *sacra doctrina* au sense de l'a. 1, de lui d'enseignement chrétien, et il entend se demander ceci : Est-ce que l'enseignement chrétien est tel qu'il a la forme et vérifie la qualité d'une science ? Il ne s'agit pas d'identifier, sans plus, enseignement chrétien et science, car l'enseignement révélé comporte bien des aspects ou des actes qui n'appartiennent pas à l'ordre de la science ; mais il s'agit de savoir si l'enseignement chrétien, au moins en l'une de ses fonctions, en l'une de ses activités, en l'un de ses actes, peut vérifier la qualité et mériter le nom de science. A cette question, saint Thomas répond affirmativement et, dans la *Somme* tout au moins, il se contente pour cela de dire que la *sacra doctrina* vérifie la qualité de science selon cette catégorie, étudiée et définie par Aristote, des sciences subalternées.
(5) M.-J. CONGAR, O.P., *Bulletin Thomiste*, V (1938-1939), pp. 495-496.

avec elle l'Écriture sainte et tous les modes d'enseignement de la foi chrétienne : non seulement l'expression *sacra doctrina* se maintient jusqu'à la fin de la question, non seulement le mot de *theologia* n'y apparait que deux fois (et encore, pas avec un sens vraiment technique), mais, dans le cours d'un même raisonnement, *sacra doctrina* et *sacra scriptura* sont pris l'un pour l'autre (par ex. à l'art. 3). L'étude du vocabulaire rend manifeste que *sacra doctrina* a, d'un bout à l'autre de la question, un même sens, et que ce sens est celui que l'expression a dans l'article 1, le sens d'enseignement surnaturel, enseignement procédant de la Révélation (1). Bien des difficultés tombent quand on a cette équivalence dans l'esprit; en particulier, la controverse classique qui oppose sur ce point les commentateurs de St. Thomas n'a plus d'objet. Rien n'empêche, d'ailleurs, qu'on distingue des parties à l'intérieur de cet enseignement surnaturel; l'expressions employées par St. Thomas (*Scriptura huius doctrinae*, art. 10; *theologia quae ad sacram doctrinam pertinet*, art. 1, ad 2m) pourraient, semble-t-il, y inviter, et il n'y a pour nous aucun doute que, si S. Thomas a compris la théologie proprement dite *et* l'Écriture à l'intérieur de la *sacra doctrina*, il n'en a pas moins, dans cette première question, parfaitement distingué la condition et la méthode de chacune.

In my opinion Fr. Congar in his article « Théologie » in the *Dictionnaire* and in his reviews in the *Bulletin Thomiste* has done more to clarify the notion of theology according to St. Thomas and the meaning of *sacra doctrina* than any other author. His interpretation of *sacra doctrina* as Christian instruction, instruction proceeding from divine revelation, represents a definite advance toward the precise definition of the term as used by St. Thomas. However, our investigation will show, I think, that he understands the term Christian instruction in too broad a sense, in making it include Sacred Scripture and theology properly so called. Sacred Scripture, sacred doctrine, and the habit of sacred theology are distinct realities in a causal series proceeding from God, man's principal teacher, and terminating in the disciple's habit of acquired supernatural wisdom. Sacred docrine itself is the action of a teacher received in a disciple terminating in the knowledge of salvation. Sacred Scripture is one of the instrumental causes of this action; the habit of acquired supernatural wisdom is the term of this action when it is adequately received by man here on earth.

Thus Sacred Scripture and the habit of sacred theology are not parts distinguished at the interior of sacred doctrine, as Fr. Congar says. Rather Scripture is related to sacred doctrine as one of its external instruments; it pertains to the efficient cause of sacred doctrine. The habit of sacred theology is related to sacred doctrine as its proportioned final cause. Sacred doctrine itself is an action proceeding ultimately from God as principal cause, received in man through the instrumentality of human teachers and their verbal and written discourse, some of which is immediately inspired, and terminating successively in faith, understanding, and wisdom, according to the measure in which this action is received. Sacred doctrine can be defined as instruction in divine knowledge by way of revelation.

In the course of the following chapters we shall see the full explanation of this interpretation and how it emerges from a consideration of the text of St. Thomas.

I think that now our investigation of the various opinions concerning the meaning of *sacra doctrina* is sufficiently complete. The following chart will serve as a summary of the opinions we have considered.

CAJETAN: *Revealed knowledge prescinding from its specification as faith or theology.*

SYLVIUS, Billuart, Sertillanges: *The science of theology.*

JOHN OF ST. THOMAS: art. 1   *Theology as doctrine*
                        art. 2-7 *Theology as science*
                        art. 8-9 *Theology as doctrine.*

GARRIGOU-LAGRANGE: art. 1   (*a*) Cf. Cajetan.
                                (*b*) *Faith.*
                                (*c*) *Theology as science.*
                      art. 2-7 *Theology as science.*
                      art. 8-9 (?)

CHENU, Gagnebet (?): *An ambiguous term* having a general sense of revelation, a technical sense of theological science, as well as a scriptural sense. Its various meanings cannot be parceled out to particular questions.

BONNEFOY: *The body of immediately revealed truths imposed on our faith.*

CONGAR: *Instruction proceeding from divine revelation.*

CHAPTER TWO

THE MEANING OF *DOCTRINA* IN ST. THOMAS

To come to a better understanding of St. Thomas' use of the term *sacra doctrina*, let us look, first of all, into the discussions which he has had concerning the term *doctrina*. His comment on Aristotle's use of the words *doctrina* and *disciplina* in the *Posterior Analytics* is very interesting both from the point of view of what he says about these terms and of how he investigates Aristotle's use of them. Moreover, this is the text from which John of St. Thomas, Fr. Gagnebet, and others derive the meaning of the term *doctrina* in St. Thomas.

... Primo, inducit universalem propositionem propositum continentem, scilicet quod acceptio cognitionis in nobis fit ex aliqua praeexistenti cognitione. Et ideo dicit: *Omnis doctrina* et *omnis disciplina,* non autem *omnis cognitio,* quia non omnis cognitio ex priori cognitione dependent: esset enim in infinitum abire. Nomen autem doctrinae et disciplinae ad cognitionis acquisitionem pertinet. Nam doctrina est actio eius, qui aliquid cognoscere facit; disciplina autem est receptio cognitionis ab alio. Non autem accipitur hic doctrina et disciplina secundum quod se habent ad acquisitionem scientiae tantum, sed ad acquisitionem cognitionis cuiuscumque. Quod patet, quia manifestat hanc propositionem etiam in disputativis et rhetoricis disputationibus, per quas non acquiritur scientia. Propter quod etiam non dicit ex praeexistenti *scientia* vel *intellectu,* sed universaliter cognitione. Addit autem intellectiva ad excludendum acceptionem cognitionis sensitivae vel imaginativae. Nam procedere ex uno in aliud rationis est solum [1].

In this text after indicating the universal proposition in which Aristotle finds the point he is trying to prove, St. Thomas shows first of all why Aristotle used the term *doctrina* and *disciplina*

---

(1) *In I Post. Anal.,* cap. 1, lect. 1 (ed. Leon., I, p. 140).

instead of *cognitio*. And this he does, first, by indicating the nominal meaning of the terms ; and secondly, by investigating the context in which they are used.

The terms *doctrina* and *disciplina*, if we look to their nominal meaning, refer to the acquisition of knowledge. *Doctrina* is the action of a person who causes knowledge in another. *Disciplina* is the reception of knowledge from another.

The terms as used in this context do not of themselves refer to the acquisition of knowledge which is science, but to the acquisition of any sort of knowledge. This is clear from the context, because Aristotle illustrates the proposition by reference to rhetorical disputations wherein no science is acquired. Moreover, this is the reason why he does not say *ex praeexistenti scientia vel intellectu* but *ex praeexistenti cognitione.*

From this text we learn, first of all, what St. Thomas regards as the nominal meaning of the term *doctrina :* i. e. the action of a person who causes knowledge in another. For this nominal meaning of the term he is not appealing merely to Aristotle, as is evident, but to what the term means in ordinary usage, « per quem est ius et norma loquendi » [1]. Secondly, we learn that the term can, at least in a given context, refer to the communication of knowledge of any sort, not merely scientific knowledge. Thirdly we learn from the example of St. Thomas to go to the context of the term to find out how it is used in a particular instance.

St. Thomas' own treatment on the nature of doctrine is found in one of his early works, *Quaestiones Disputatae De Veritate*, question 11, *De Magistro* (1256-1259). It is a masterpiece. Somehow this *locus classicus* was overlooked by Schütz in his *Thomas Lexikon* [2] and also by the editors of the new dictionary of St. Thomas, *A Lexicon of St. Thomas Aquinas* [3]. This treatise consists of only four articles : 1) *Utrum homo possit docere et dici magister vel solus Deus ?* 2) *Utrum aliquis possit dici magister sui ipsius ?* 3) *Utrum homo ab angelo doceri possit ?* 4) *Utrum docere sit actus vitae activae vel contemplativae ?*

(1) HORACE, *Ars Poetica*.
(2) LUDWIG SCHÜTZ, *Thomas Lexikon*[2]. Paderborn: Ferdinand Schöningh, 1895.
(3) R. J. DEFERRARI, PH. D., SISTER M. INVIOLATA BARRY, C.D.P., IGNATIUS McGUINESS, O.P., *A Lexicon of St. Thomas Aquinas based on the Summa Theologica and selected passages from his other works*. Washington, D. C. : The Catholic University of America Press, - Fascicle I : A-C, 1948 ; Fascicle II : D-H, 1949 ; Fascicle III : I-M, 1949 ; Fascicle IV : N-Q, 1949 (Five fascicles to appear).

This treatise appears to be the first of its kind in the Middle Ages. For anything similar in character it seems that we have to go back to St. Augustine [1]. The questions of the possibility of one man teaching another and of the sense in which man can be called a teacher are questions which seem to be peculiar to St. Thomas. At least, we do not find such questions discussed by St. Albert nor by any of the other predecessors of St. Thomas in the Middle Ages [2]. This fact may be of considerable importance in explaining the full historical significance to be attached to the consistent use of the term *sacra doctrina* in preference to *theologia* in the *Summa Theologica* of St. Thomas. However, as this study is limited to a consideration of the term *sacra doctrina* in the works of St. Thomas himself, we shall not endeavor to develop this point here.

The matter of the first article of the treatise *De Magistro* is treated again by St. Thomas in the *Summa contra Gentiles*, Bk. II, c. 75 (1261-1264) and also in the *Summa Theologica*, I, 117, 1, (1266). And we find a summary treatment of the same in Opusculum XVI, *De Unitate Intellectus*, c. 5, (1270).

Thomas' first delineation however, of the meaning of *doctrina* appears in the *Com. in II Sent.*, dist. 9, q. 1, a. 2, ad 4 [3]. In this

(1) ST. AUGUSTINE, *De Magistro. PL* 32, 1193-1220.
(2) Cf. P. GLORIEUX, *Répertoire des maîtres en théologie de Paris au XIIIᵉ siècle.* 2 vols. (Études de philosophie médiévale, XVII-XVIII). Paris: J. Vrin, 1933.
ID., *La littérature quodlibétique.* 2 vols. (Bibliothèque thomiste, V, XXI). Vol. I: — *La littérature quodlibétique de 1260 à 1320.* Kain (Belgique): Le Saulchoir, 1925, pp. 382. Vol. II: *La littérature quodlibétique.* Paris: J. Vrin, 1925, pp. 387.
ID., « Les 572 Questions du manuscrit de Douai 434 », *Recherches de Théologie Ancienne et Médiévale*, X (1938), pp. 123-152, 225-267.
O. LOTTIN, O.S.B., « Quelques 'Quaestiones' de maîtres parisiens aux environs de 1225-1235 », *Recherches de Théol. Anc. et Méd.*, V (1933) pp. 79-95.
FREDERICUS STEGMÜLLER, *Repertorium Commentariorum in Sententias Petri Lombardi*. 2 vols., Herbipoli (Würzburg): apud Ferd. Schöningh, Bibliopolam, 1947.
(3) — ... Vel dicendum quod docere proprie dicitur qui in cognitionem rei ducit. Sicut autem in cognitionem coloris sensibilem pervenit homo ex duobus, scilicet ex visibili obiecto, et ex lumine sub quo videtur, unde et uterque dicitur demonstare rem, scilicet qui lumen praeparat, et qui obiectum repraesentat, ita etiam ad cognitionem intellectualem duo exiguntur: scilicet ipsum intelligibile, et lumen per quod videtur; et ideo dupliciter dicitur aliquis docere, vel sicut proponens intelligibile, vel sicut praebens lumen ad intelligendum. Hoc autem lumen est duplex. Unum intrinsecum vel connaturale intellectui, cui similatur lumen quod est de compositione oculi; et per collationem huius luminis solus Deus docere dicitur. Secundum lumen est superveniens² ad conformationem connaturalis luminis, cui similatur in visu corporali lumen solis vel candelae; et sic potest angelus alium angelum vel etiam hominem illuminare ad aliquid cognoscendum. Non autem homo sic docere potest, cum in eo lumen intellectuale debilissime recipiatur. Quidam tamen dicunt quod nullo modo angelus docet sicut

text St. Thomas is answering the objection that only God illuminates the mind of an angel, and so one angel cannot illuminate another. He gives two answers to the objection : first, the traditional answer, and secondly, an answer based on the diverse ways in which God, angels, and men are said to teach.

To teach, he says, is properly said of a person who leads another to the knowledge of something. Just as man's sensible knowledge of color results from two principles, the visible object and the light under which it is seen, so that both he who prepares the light and he who presents the object are said to manifest the object, so two principles are required for intellectual knowledge, namely the intelligible object and the light in which it is seen.

Hence a person can be said to teach in two ways : either by proposing the intelligible object or by affording the light by which the object is seen. This light, however, is twofold : one which is intrinsic or connatural to the intellect. To it can be likened the light which belongs to the composition of the eye. Only God can be said to teach by way of affording this connatural light. The second light is one superadded to strengthen the connatural light. To this can be likened the light of the sun or of a candle in corporal vision. With this superadded light one angel can illuminate another angel or even a man to the knowledge of something. Man, however, is incapable of teaching in this way, because of the weakness of the intellectual light which he has received. Some, however, deny that angels can teach by affording light in any way. This, however, seems to be expressly contrary to what Dionysius says in his *De caelesti hierarchia*.

The intelligible object is likewise twofold : one which the intellect of some man is capable of knowing provided only that it be proposed to his consideration. Hence the person who proposes such an object is said to teach by leading the other, as it were,

lumen praebens; quod expresse dictis DIONYSII, *De cael. hier.*, c. X, col. 271, t. I, contrariari videtur. Similiter etiam intelligibile duplex est. Unum ad quod intelligendum sufficit intellectus alicuius hominis, dummodo sibi considerandum proponatur; unde et ipse proponens docere dicitur quasi in cognitionem ducens, sicut in visu corporali monstrat rem qui eam coram oculis ponit. Aliud est ad cuius cognitionem non sufficit intellectus discipuli, nisi in hoc manuducatur per aliquid sibi magis [1] notum : unde et qui hoc magis notum sibi proponit, docere eum dicitur. Huius simile est in visu corporali in hoc quod aliquis alicui rem a longe apparentem digito monstrat; et his duobus modis homo docere dicitur; et haec doctrina est non per modum illuminationis, sed per modum locutionis.

to knowledge, just as in sensible vision one who presents an object before the eyes of another manifests it. The other intelligible object is one for the knowledge of which the intellect of the disciple is not sufficient unless he be led by the hand, as it were, through something which is better known to him. Hence also one who proposes this [better known][1] object is said to teach. There is some similarity here to corporal vision, when someone points out to another with his finger something appearing in the distance.

In these two ways man is said to teach. And this doctrine does not take place by way of illumination, but by way of speech.

Thus man can be said to teach in two ways: first by proposing some object which need only be presented to the consideration of the disciple to be known. The intellect of the disciple in this case has sufficient power to know the object without being led by the hand, as it were, through the operation of knowledge.

This does not mean necessarily that the object is immediately evident, but that once the object is presented, even if some reasoning and reduction to principles is required, the disciple has the power to understand it without being put through the operation of reason by the teacher.

Secondly, men can teach by proposing some object for the understanding of which the disciple must be led through a medium or middle term which is better known to the disciple. In this case the intellect of the disciple does not have the collative power of intellect necessary to perform the operation of reason required to understand it, but must be put through the operation by the teacher.

In either case, however, the process takes place by way of speech.

Later on in the *Commentary* St. Thomas describes again for us the work of teaching[2]. Here he is answering the objection that man cannot know any truth without grace, because no one can learn unless God teach him interiorly. It is interesting to see Tho-

(1) There seems to be a corruption of the text here.
(2) *In II Sent.*, d. 28, q. 1, a. 5, ad 3: — Ad tertium dicendum, quod sicut dicit AUGUSTINUS, I *De doct. christ.*, in prologo, § 3, col. 16, t. III, ille qui docet, similis est ei qui movet digitum ad aliquid ostendendum: unde sicut homo potest exterius movere digitum ut aliquid ostendat, non autem potest conferre virtutem visivam, per quam ille qui docetur doctrinam visibilem advertat, ita etiam potest homo exterius verba proferre, quae sunt signa veritatis, non tamen veri intelligendi virtutem praebere, quae a solo Deo est. Pro tanto ergo dicitur ipse solus Deus docere, quia vim intelligendi in nobis continet et causat; non ex hoc quod in qualibet cognitione veritatis novum lumen gratiae superinfundat...

mas returning for his explanation to the same example from corporal vision which he found in St. Augustine's work, *De Doctrina Christiana.*

He who teaches, he says, is like one who moves his finger to point out something to another. So just as man can externally move his finger to point out something but cannot confer the power of vision with which he who is being taught takes notice of this visible teaching, so also man can externally utter words which are signs of truth but cannot confer the power of knowing the truth which comes from God alone. Therefore in this sense is God alone said to teach, because He contains and causes in us the power of understanding ; not because there is a new light of grace superadded in every act of knowledge.

In the *De Magistro* the first article deals with the question whether man, or only God, can be said to teach and be called a teacher. In this text the question is discussed primarily in the context of the acquisition of science, although St. Thomas here also allows for the teaching of knowledges which are not science.

In the body of the article he notes, first of all, that there is the same diversity of opinion in regard to three questions : how forms are educed, the acquisition of virtues, and the acquisition of sciences. For the same principles are involved in the solution of all three problems. After briefly explaining the opinion of Avicenna and that of the Platonists and showing them to be incongruous, he proposes the teaching of Aristotle as the one to be accepted on all three of the above questions [1].

---

(1) *Ver.* 11. 1c. : — Formae enim naturales praeexistunt quidem in materia, non in actu, ut alii dicebant, sed in potentia solum, de qua in actum reducitur per agens extrinsecum proximum non solum per agens primum, ut alia opinio ponebat.

Similiter etiam secundum ipsius sententiam in VI *Ethicorum* [II], virtutum habitus ante earum consummationem praeexistunt in nobis in quibusdam naturalibus inclinationibus, quae sunt quaedam virtutum inchoationes, sed postea per exercitium operum adducuntur in debitam consummationem.

Similiter etiam dicendum est de scientiae acquisitione ; quod praeexistunt in nobis quaedam scientiarum semina, scilicet primae conceptiones intellectus, quae statim lumine intellectus agentis cognoscuntur per species a sensibilibus abstractas, sive sint complexa, ut dignitates, sive incomplexa, sicut ratio entis, et unius, et huiusmodi, quae statim intellectus apprehendit. Ex istis autem principiis universalibus omnia principia sequuntur, sicut ex quibusdam rationibus seminalibus. Quando ergo ex istis universalibus cognitionibus mens educitur ut actu cognoscat particularia, quae prius in potentia, et quasi in universali cognoscebantur, tunc aliquis dicitur scientiam acquirere.

E) Sciendum tamen est, quod in naturalibus rebus aliquid praeexistit in potentia *dupliciter.*

Uno modo in potentia activa completa ; quando, scilicet, principium intrin-

Natural forms pre-exist in matter only in potency. They are reduced to act by a proximate external agent as well as by the first agent. The case is similar for the acquisition of the virtues.

Likewise there pre-exist in us certain seeds of science, namely the first conceptions of the intellect which are immediately known with the light of the agent intellect through species abstracted from

secum sufficienter potest perducere in actum perfectum, sicut patet in sanatione : ex virtute enim naturali quae est in aegro, aeger ad sanitatem perducitur.

Alio modo in potentia passiva; quando, scilicet, principium intrinsecum non sufficit ad educendum in actum, sicut patet quando ex aëre fit ignis ; hoc enim non potest fieri per aliquam virtutem in aërem existentem.

Quando igitur praeexistit aliquid in potentia activa completa, tunc agens extrinsecum non agit nisi adiuvando agens intrinsecum, et ministrando ei ea quibus possit in actum exire ; sicut medicus in sanatione est minister naturae, quae principaliter operatur, confortando naturam, et apponendo medicinas, quibus velut instrumentis natura utitur ad sanationem.

Quando vero aliquid praeexistit in potentia passiva tantum, tunc agens extrinsecum est quod educit principaliter de potentia in actum ; sicut ignis facit de aëre, qui est potentia ignis, actu ignem.

Scientia ergo praeexistit in addiscente in potentia non pure passiva, sed activa ; alias homo non posset per seipsum acquirere scientiam.

F) Sicut ergo aliquis *dupliciter* sanatur ; *uno modo* per operationem naturae tantum, *alio modo* a natura cum adminiculo medicinae ; ita etiam est *duplex* modus acquirendi scientiam : *unus,* quando naturalis ratio per seipsam devenit in cognitionem ignotorum ; et hic modus dicitur *inventio* ; *alius,* quando rationi naturali aliquis exterius adminiculatur, et hic modus dicitur *disciplina*.

In his autem quae fiunt a natura et arte, eodem modo operatur ars, et per eadem media, quibus et natura. Sicut enim natura in eo qui ex frigida causa laborat, calefaciendo induceret sanitatem, ita et medicus ; unde et ars dicitur imitari naturam. Similiter etiam contingit in scientiae acquisitione, quod eodem modo docens alium ad scientiam ignotorum ducit sicuti aliquis inveniendo deducit seipsum in cognitionem ignoti.

Processus autem rationis pervenientis ad cognitionem ignoti in inveniendo est ut principia communia per se nota applicet ad determinatas materias, et inde procedat in aliquas particulares conclusiones, et ex his in alias ; unde et secundum hoc unus alium docere dicitur, quod istum discursum rationis, quem in se facit ratione naturali, alteri exponit per signa et sic ratio naturalis discipuli, per huiusmodi sibi proposita, sicut per quaedam instrumenta, pervenit in cognitionem ignotorum.

Sicut ergo medicus dicitur causare sanitatem in infirmo natura operante, ita etiam homo dicitur causare scientiam in alio operatione rationis naturalis illius ; et hoc est docere ; unde unus homo alium docere dicitur, et eius esse magister. Et secundum hoc dicit Philosophus, I *Posteriorum* [comm. 51], quod demonstratio est syllogismus faciens scire.

Si autem aliquis alicui proponat ea quae in principiis per se notis non includuntur, vel includi non manifestantur, non faciet in eo scientiam, sed forte opinionem, vel fidem, quamvis etiam hoc aliquo modo ex principiis innatis causetur. Ex ipsis enim principiis per se notis considerat, quod ea quae ex eis necessario consequuntur, sunt certitudinaliter tenenda ; quae vero eis sunt contraria, totaliter respuenda ; aliis autem assensum praebere potest, vel non.

Huiusmodi autem rationis lumen, quo principia huiusmodi sunt nobis certa, est nobis a Deo inditum, quasi quaedam similitudo increatae veritatis in nobis resultantis. Unde, cum omnis doctrina humana efficaciam habere non possit nisi ex virtute illius luminis, constat quod solus Deus est qui interius et principaliter docet, sicut natura interius etiam principaliter sanat ; nihilominus tamen et sanare et docere proprie dicitur modo praedicto.

matter. These first conceptions may be either complex, as the first complex principles, or incomplex, as the notion of being, and of one, and so forth, which the intellect grasps immediately. From these universal principles all other principles proceed as if from certain seeds of reason. So when from these universal knowledges the mind is led to actual knowledge of particular things which are previously known only in potency and, as it were, in general, then someone is said to acquire science.

Now something pre-exists potentially in natural things in a twofold manner. First, it pre-exists in complete active potency, when the intrinsic principle is sufficient to reduce what is in potency to perfect act, as is clear in the case of the restoration of health. The sick man is restored to health through the natural virtue which is in him. Secondly, it pre-exists in passive potency, when the intrinsic principle is not sufficient for the reduction to act, as is clear when from air fire is produced. For this does not result from any virtue existing in the air.

When, therefore, something pre-exists in complete active potency, then the extrinsic agent does nothing but assist the intrinsic principle and administer to it that with which it can pass into act. For example, a doctor in effecting a cure is the minister of nature which is the principal agent; he aids it and gives medicines which nature uses as instruments of the cure.

But when something pre-exists only in passive potency, the external agent is the principal cause of the reduction from potency to act. In this way fire produces fire from the air which is potentially fire.

Science, then, pre-exists in the student potentially, not in mere passive potency, but active; otherwise man could not acquire science by himself.

Now just as there are two ways of restoring health, one through the operation of nature alone, the other from nature with the help of medicine, so there are two ways of acquiring science, one when natural reason by itself comes to the knowledge of the unknown, and this is called discovery; the other when the natural reason receives external aid, and this is called discipline.

In regard to those effects which are produced by nature and art together, art operates in the same manner and with the same means as nature. Just as in one who is suffering from the cold, nature effects its cure by warming him up, so too does the doctor.

Hence art is said to imitate nature. Likewise in the acquisition of science, the teacher leads the disciple to the knowledge of the unknown in the same manner as the student leads himself by discovery to the knowledge of the unknown.

The process of reason by which one arrives at the knowledge of the unknown through discovery consists in applying the common principles which are immediately known to determined matter and then proceeding to some particular conclusions, and from these conclusions to others. Hence one is said to teach another in so far as he proposes by means of signs that discourse of reason which he himself performs with his natural reason, and in this way the disciple by means of what is proposed to him as instrumental aids arrives at the knowledge of the unknown.

So just as the doctor is said to restore health in a sick person through the operation of nature, so a man is said to cause science in another through the operation of the nature of his disciple. And this is to teach. So it is that one man is said to teach another and to be a teacher. And it is in this regard that the Philosopher says that demonstration is a syllogism causing science.

If, however, someone proposes to another some truths which are not included in self-evident principles, or which are not demonstrated from such principles, he does not cause science in the other, but perhaps opinion or faith although even this knowledge is in some way caused by innate principles. For the one learning such truths considers that whatever necessarily follows from these self-evident principles is to be held for certain; what is contrary to them is to be rejected; and to what neither follows from them nor is contrary to them he can give his consent or refuse it.

This light of reason, by which principles are known to us, is bestowed on us by God and is a certain likeness of divine truth resulting in us. Hence, since all human teaching has its efficacy only in virtue of that light, it is clear that only God teaches interiorly and as principal agent, just as nature interiorly and as principal agent restores one to health. Nevertheless it is proper to speak of curing and of teaching in the manner explained above.

According to St. Thomas, therefore, to teach in human fashion means to lead a disciple to new knowledge through a discourse which is the intellectual operation of the disciple himself but caused externally by a teacher proposing this discourse through the instrumentality of words. This discourse in the disciple is the movement of the intellect from potential to actual knowledge. In the acquisition of sciences this discourse is represented in demonstration.

In the answer to the eleventh objection [1] St. Thomas elucidates the function of the words of the teacher in causing science in the disciple. In the disciple, he says, intelligible forms are described, out of which the science which was received by way of teaching (*doctrina*) is constituted; immediately, by the agent intellect, and mediately, by the teacher. For the teacher proposes signs of intelligible objects from which the agent intellect fashions intelligible species in the possible intellect. Hence the words of the teacher which are heard or which are seen in writing have the same function in causing a science as things which exist outside the mind, because from both the intellect receives intelligible species. Yet the words of the teacher are more proximate in their causality of science than sensible things existing outside the mind, in so far as words are signs of intelligible species.

However, the proximate cause of science is not these words or signs, but the discourse itself of reason from principles to conclusions [2].

In answer to the 12th objection [3] St. Thomas elucidates still

(1) *Ver.*, 11, 1, ad 11 : — Ad undecimum dicendum, quod in discipulo describuntur formae intelligibiles, ex quibus scientia per doctrinam accepta constituitur, immediate quidem per intellectum agentem, sed mediate per eum qui docet. Proponit enim doctor rerum intelligibilium signa ex quibus intellectus agens accipit intentiones intelligibiles, et describit eas in intellectu possibili. Unde ipsa verba doctoris audita, vel visa in scripta, hoc modo se habent ad causandum scientiam in intellectu sicut res quae sunt extra animam, quia ex utrisque intellectus intentiones intelligibiles accipit; quamvis verba doctoris propinquius se habeant ad causandum scientiam quam sensibilia extra animam existentia inquantum sunt signa intelligibilium intentionum.

(2) *Ver.*, 11, 1, ad 4 : — Ad quartum dicendum, quod ex sensibilibus signis, quae in potentia sensitiva recipiuntur, intellectus accipit intentiones intelligibiles quibus utitur ad scientiam in seipso faciendam. Proximum enim scientiae effectivum non sunt signa, sed ratio discurrens a principiis in conclusiones, ut dictum est, in corpore articuli.

(3) *Ver.*, 11, 1, ad 12 : — Ad duodecimum dicendum, quod non est simile de intellectu et visu corporali. Visus enim corporalis non est vis collativa, ut ex quibusdam suorum obiectorum in alia perveniat : sed omnia sua obiecta sunt ei visibilia, quam cito ad illa convertitur : unde habens potentiam visivam se habet hoc modo ad omnia visibilia intuenda, sicut habens habitum ad ea quae habitualiter scit consideranda ; et ideo videns non indiget ab alio excitari ad videndum, nisi quatenus per alium eius visus dirigitur in aliquod visibile, ut digito, vel aliquo huiusmodi.

Sed potentia intellectiva, cum sit collativa, ex quibusdam in alia devenit ; unde non se habet aequaliter ad omnia intelligibilia consideranda ; sed statim quaedam videt, ut quae sunt per se nota, in quibus implicite continentur quaedam alia quae intelligere non potest nisi per officium rationis ea quae in principiis implicite continentur, explicando ; unde ad huiusmodi cognoscenda, ante-

more the causality exercised by the teacher in teaching, from a consideration of the difference between the power of vision and the power of intellection. Corporal vision, he says, is not a collative power in the sense that from some of its objects it arrives at others; but all of its objects are visible to it from the moment the eye is turned toward them. Hence one who has the power of sight stands in relation to visible objects as one having the habit of science to the consideration of those things he habitually knows. Hence he does not need to be moved by another to the act of seeing, except in so far as his sight is directed toward something visible.

But since the intellectual power in man is collative, it proceeds from knowledge of some things to a knowledge of others, and hence it does not stand in the same relation to all the things it can consider. Some things it sees immediately, such as self-evident principles, which contain implicitly other truths which cannot be understood except through the work of reason unfolding those truths which are implicitly contained in the principles. Hence in regard to the knowledge of such things, before it has the habit of such truth, it is not only in accidental potency, but in essential potency. For it needs a cause to reduce it to act by *doctrina*, whereas he who has the habit of such truth does not need such a cause.

A teacher, therefore, excites the intellect to understand the truths he is teaching, as an essential mover reducing the intellect from potency to act. But one pointing out something to corporal vision excites it as an accidental mover, just as one having the habit of science could be excited to the consideration of something.

It is clear from this text that if the intellect of the disciple is perfectly equipped to know the object presented, such as is the case in regard to self-evident principles and objects of a science the habit of which is already possessed by the listener, the teacher functions only as a *motor accidentalis* in causing the knowledge of such objects in the listener. It is not the essential function of a teacher to teach such knowledge.

quam habitum habeat, non solum est in potentia accidentali, sed etiam in potentia essentiali; indiget enim motore, qui reducat eum in actum per doctrinam ut dicitur in VIII Physic. [comm. 32]: quo non indiget ille qui habitualiter iam aliquid novit.

Doctor ergo excitat intellectum ad sciendum illa quae docet, sicut motor essentialis educens de potentia in actum; sed ostendens rem aliquam visui corporali, excitat eum sicut motor per accidens; prout etiam habens habitum scientiae potest excitari ad considerandum de aliquo.

If, however, the intellect of the listener is not perfectly equipped to know the objects presented by the teacher, the teacher then functions as a *motor essentialis*. In this case we may note two possibilities which St. Thomas takes up in a later text [1]. The first is that of a disciple who has sufficient collative power of intellect to resolve the propositions presented into principles already known to him. The second is that of a disciple who may not have sufficient collative power of intellect to make this reduction to principles or deduction from principles unless the teacher puts the disciple through this operation by proposing the order of principles to conclusions.

To this twofold intellectual disposition on the part of the disciple corresponds the twofold manner of teaching spoken of in the *Commentary on the Sentences* [2] which receives greater clarification in the *Summa* [3].

We can see a reason why in this treatise St. Thomas discusses primarily the function of a teacher in causing science in his disciple. For in presenting the objects of a science not yet acquired, the teacher functions as a *per se* cause of the knowledge to be acquired by the disciple, whereas in presenting an object of knowledge which is self-evident or an object of a science already acquired by the disciple, the teacher functions only as a cause *per accidens* of the resulting knowledge. Now just as in any science what is *per se* is taken up for consideration and what is *per accidens* is left aside, except for purposes of illustration [4], so also in this treatise on the function of the human teacher.

It should be noted, however, that in speaking of science as the object of teaching in this article, St. Thomas is using the term to signify any certain actual knowledge derived by a process of reasoning from universal principles, wherein the intellect applies the self-evident common principles to a determinate matter and proceeds to conclusions and from these conclusions to others. Now this is the case in all sciences, whether they are *scientiae propter quid* or *scientiae quia*.

Moreover, in this article St. Thomas allows for the teaching of knowledge which may be received on faith or merely opinion.

(1) See page 68.
(2) See pages 54-55.
(3) See page 68 f.
(4) Cf. *in Boethii de Trin.*, q. 5, a. 4, ad 1.

Even in these cases, he says, the knowledge resulting is somehow caused by these common principles. What seems to be essential to the notion of teaching is the process of communicating to a disciple new knowledge which results in some manner, at least, from these common principles. Thus St. Thomas after Aristotle says that all teaching *(doctrina)* must begin from previous knowledge. Hence even in the teaching of truths to be accepted on faith, the presentation of such truths must find its starting point in knowledge previously acquired by the disciple. Moreover, in those cases where the authority of the teacher himself is the reason for accepting such truth, we notice that the causality of the teacher is enhanced, because he is not only functioning as a ministerial instrumental cause of the knowledge acquired, but in a sense as principal cause, in so far as he moves the will of the disciple to command the assent to the truth. However, in so far as the will of the disciple remains free to command or not to command the assent, teaching *(doctrina)* is more imperfect in this case because from it new and certain knowledge does not result with necessity.

In answer to the thirteenth objection [1] St. Thomas proceeds to clarify still more the function of the teacher in causing science in his disciple. Although the teacher is a cause of the science, he is not the cause of the certitude of the science. For the certitude of science is derived entirely from the certitude of the principles involved. For then only are conclusions known with certitude when they are resolved into their principles. And therefore, the understanding of something with certitude results from the light of reason with which we are endowed by God and by which God speaks to us. It does not come from man who teaches externally, except in so far as in teaching us he resolves conclusions to their principles. But even so we would not get certitude in science unless we had certitude in regard to the principles into which the conclusions are resolved.

To give a summary of the notion of teaching including only

(1) *Ver.*, 11, 1, ad 13 : — Ad decimum tertium dicendum, quod certitudo scientiae tota oritur ex certitudine principiorum : tunc enim conclusiones per certitudine sciuntur, quando resolvuntur in principia. Et ideo, quod aliquid per certitudinem sciatur, est ex lumine rationis divinitus interius indito, quo in nobis loquitur Deus : non autem ab homine exterius docente, nisi quatenus conclusiones in principia resolvit, nos docens : ex quo tamen nos certitudinem scientiae non acciperemus, nisi inesset in nobis certitudo principiorum, in quae conclusiones resolvuntur.

5

those points which certainly appear in this first article of the *De Magistro*, we may say that to teach is to reduce potential knowledge in the disciple to act, to induce in the disciple by way of verbal discourse the rational discourse which has its principle in knowledge previously acquired and its term in the new knowledge communicated.

Thus, if we should try to speak of the reality signified by the verb *to teach* in terms of its causes, we would say its efficient cause (ministerial, instrumental) is the teacher, or more proximately the verbal discourse of the teacher; its formal cause, the rational discourse in the disciple as induced by the teacher; its material cause, the disciple, or more precisely the intellect of the disciple; its final cause, the knowledge which is the term of the rational discourse in the disciple.

Docere signifies the action of teaching in the concrete, whereas *doctrina* signifies this action in the abstract [1]; just as, for example, red signifies an accident as concreted in a subject; redness an accident considered in itself, not as concreted in a subject, although it always exists in a subject. Hence *doctrina* signifies the action of teaching considered in itself, in the abstract. This action is the reduction of potential knowledge to actual knowledge. This reduction consists in the rational movement induced by the teacher in his disciple terminating in new knowledge acquired. Hence *doctrina* is formally the rational discourse induced by a teacher in his disciple terminating in new knowledge acquired.

St. Thomas, however, does not always use this term in its formal sense. Here in the first article of the *De Magistro* he uses it seven times; just once, however, in the body of the article [2].

(1) *In III Phys.* cap. 3, lect. 5 (ed. Leon. II, p. 113): — ... doctio [doctrina] et doctrina [doctrina addiscentis used here for the term disciplina] dicuntur in abstracto, docere autem et discere in concreto... (See below page 69).

(2) 1) obj. 3: — ... Si ergo homo nihil aliud faciat ad doctrinam quam signa proponere...

2) obj. 6: — ... cum doctrina nihil aliud esse videatur nisi transfusio scientiae de magistro in discipulum...

3) obj. 12: — ... per doctrinam solummodo mens hominis excitatur ad sciendum...

4) ad 6: — ... per doctrinam fit in discipulo scientia similis ei quae est in magistro, educta de potentia in actum, ...

5) ad 12: — ... indiget enim motore, qui reducat eum in actum per doctrinam, ...

6) ad 16: — ... sicut intellectus agens... quo mediante, ex rebus sensibilibus et ex doctrina hominis causatur scientia in anima nostra, ...

7) in corp.: — ... cum omnis doctrina humana efficaciam habere non possit nisi ex virtute illius luminis, ...

Although each time the term may be understood in its formal sense, in at least two instances it may also be understood as the verbal discourse of the teacher ordered to the rational discourse in the disciple [1]. This usage should not surprise us. For *doctrina* not only has its cause in the verbal discourse of the teacher, but verbal discourse is the only ordinary human way of representing this rational discourse to the disciple and even of observing it. Hence although *doctrina* exists formally only in the disciple, it exists causally and representatively in the verbal discourse of the teacher. And thus even the verbal discourse of the teacher can be called doctrine in so far as its signification as well as its effect is the rational discourse in the disciple terminating in new knowledge.

The formal character of teaching is brought out more clearly in the fourth article of the *De Magistro,* where St. Thomas discusses the question whether teaching is an act of the contemplative or of the active life. *Doctrina* here is said to consist more in the transfusion of the knowledge of things that are seen than in the vision of them, and thus the contemplative life is not *doctrina* itself but the principle of *doctrina,* just as heat is not the action of heating itself but the principle of the action.

Ad tertium dicendum, quod visio docentis est principium doctrinae ; sed ipsa doctrina magis consistit in transfusione scientiae rerum visarum quam in earum visione ; unde visio docentis magis pertinet ad actionem quam ad contemplationem.

Ad quartum dicendum, quod ratio illa probat quod vita contemplativa sit principium doctrinae ; sicut calor non est ipsa calefactio, sed calefactionis principium, in quantum eam dirigit ; sicut e converso activa vita ad contemplativam disponit.

Just as the action of heating *(calefactio)* does not formally begin until the action begins to be received into the subject, so the transfusion of knowledge in which doctrine consists does not formally begin until the action, which in this case is the rational discourse, begins in the disciple.

This formal signification of the term *doctrina* was sufficiently indicated in the first article, both in the consideration of teaching as a reduction of the intellect of the disciple from potential to

(1) See previous note, 3) and 6).

actual knowledge and in the key sentence of the article: ... *homo dicitur causare scientiam in alio operatione rationis naturalis illius; et hoc est docere ;* ... The human teacher teaches as an external cause, externally with words. His verbal discourse not only signifies the rational discourse which he induces in the disciple, but it is the instrument of this action in which *doctrina* formally consists. As early as the *Commentary on the Sentences* St. Thomas makes this distinction between the verbal discourse of the teacher and *doctrina: ... haec doctrina est... per modum locutionis* [1]. Thus already in his earliest works we find at least implicitly what in his later works becomes explicit: *scientia acquiritur per doctrinam ; doctrina est generatio scientiae ; doctrina fit per locutionem.*

In the *Summa contra Gentiles*, II, 75 (1261-1264) St. Thomas explains in more detail how the teacher proceeds in presenting this rational discourse to the disciple. This discussion about teaching comes up in the refutation of Averroes' opinion about the unity of the possible intellect. One of the arguments offered by Averroes to prove the unity of the possible intellect in all men is from the nature of *doctrina*, as Averroes conceived it.

Science in the teacher and in the disciple, says Averroes, is numerically one and the same science. For it must be either numerically the same, or numerically different though specifically the same. However, the second alternative seems impossible, because then the teacher would cause science in his disciple in the same way that he produces his form in another, by generation of its specific likeness ; this mode of causality, however, appears to belong to material agents. Hence science in teacher and disciple must be numerically one. But this is impossible unless the possible intellect of both be numerically one.

A very interesting study would consist in investigating whether other Scholastics of the Middle Ages in refuting the doctrine of Averroes on the unity of the possible intellect have handled this argument in particular and how they have handled it.

To show the invalidity of this argument St. Thomas is forced to discuss how the causality involved in teaching which is *per modum artis* differs from causality which is *per modum naturae*. He has done this before. However, here he explains in more detail the discourse by which the teacher reduces the potential knowledge of the disciple to act.

(1) *In II Sent.*, d. 9, q. 1, a. 2, ad 4.

Science, he says[1], is acquired in two ways: by discovery without teaching (*inventio*), and by teaching (*doctrina*). A teacher, therefore, begins to teach in the way that discovery proceeds. He offers to the consideration of the disciple the principles known to him, because all discipline and science has its origin in pre-existing knowledge. He draws conclusions from these principles. And he proposes examples from the sensible order from which the phantasms necessary for understanding are formed in the mind of the disciple. And because the external operation of the teacher would have no effect without the intrinsic principle of science, which is in us from God, it is therefore said among theologians that man teaches by external ministration and God by internal operation, just as the doctor is said to be the minister of nature in effecting a cure. Thus science is caused by the teacher in the disciple not by way of natural but artificial action.

Here it is clear what St. Thomas means by *doctrina*. Science is acquired by discovery or by teaching. Discovery is a natural action, the natural discourse in the student by which he acquires science by himself. Teaching (*doctrina*) is an artificial action; it is the rational discourse induced artificially (*per modum artis*) by the teacher in the disciple.

We might compare discovery and teaching with natural respiration and artificial respiration. Discovery and natural respiration are natural actions, operations by which unaided nature achieves certain effects. Teaching (*doctrina*) and artificial respiration are artificial actions, operations by which nature as internal cause and art as external minister of nature achieve the same effects as unaided nature does by discovery and natural respiration.

If artificial respiration consisted formally in a certain movement of the hands on the back of the body and not in the vital movement induced in the patient by this movement of the hands, a

(1) *Summa contra Gentiles*, II, 75 : — ... et ideo scientia acquiritur dupliciter : et sine doctrina per inventionem, et per doctrinam. Docens igitur hoc modo incipit docere sicut inveniens incipit invenire, offerendo scilicet considerationi discipuli principia ab eo nota ; quia omnis disciplina et omnis scientia ab prae-existenti fit cognitione, et illa principia in conclusiones deducendo, et proponendo exempla sensibilia ex quibus in anima discipuli formentur phantasmata necessaria ad intelligendum. Et quia exterior operatio docentis nihil operaretur nisi adesset principium intrinsecum scientiae, quod inest nobis divinitus, ideo apud theologos dicitur quod homo docet ministerium exhibendo, Deus autem interius operando ; sicut et medicus dicitur naturae minister in sanando. Sic igitur causatur scientia in discipulo per magistrum, non modo naturalis actionis, sed artificialis, ut dictum est.

person could be said to be giving artificial respiration whether his patient were a man or a mummy. Likewise if teaching consisted formally in the verbal discourse of a teacher and not in the rational discourse induced in his disciple, a man could be said to be teaching even if all his disciples were asleep before him. We know, however, that if all his disciples are asleep before him, he is not teaching anybody anything. He is simply not teaching. Hence teaching cannot consist formally in the verbal discourse of the teacher. It is an artificial action proceeding from a teacher but received in his disciple.

In the *Summa Theologica* (Pars Prima, 1266)[1] the method by which the teacher leads the disciple to new knowledge is explained in more detail. The teacher does this in a twofold way. The first method consists in proposing to the disciple some helps or instruments which the intellect of the disciple uses in acquiring the science. For example, he proposes some propositions which are less universal and which the disciple can resolve into what is already known to him. Or he proposes some examples from the sensible order, which are analogous or opposite or something of the sort, from which the intellect of the disciple is led along by the hand, as it were, to the knowledge of the unknown truth. The second method consists in giving support to the intellect of the disciple. This is done by proposing to the disciple the order of principles to conclusions, because perhaps the disciple by himself does not have sufficient collative power to be able to deduce conclusions from the principles[2]. For this reason Aristotle says that demonstration is a syllogism causing science. And

(1) *Summa Theologica*, I, 117, 1c : — Ducit autem magister discipulum ex praecognitis in cognitionem ignotorum dupliciter. Primo quidem, proponendo ei aliqua auxilia vel instrumenta, quibus intellectus eius utatur ad scientiam acquirendam ; puta cum proponit ei aliquas propositiones minus universales, quas tamen ex praecognitis discipulus diiudicare potest ; vel cum proponit ei aliqua sensibilia exempla, vel similia, vel opposita, vel aliqua huiusmodi, ex quibus intellectus addiscentis manuducitur in cognitionem veritatis ignotae. Alio modo, cum confortat intellectum addiscentis ; non quidem aliqua virtute activa quasi superioris naturae, sicut supra dictum est de angelis illuminantibus, quia omnes humani intellectus sunt unius gradus in ordine naturae, sed inquantum proponit discipulo ordinem principiorum ad conclusiones, qui forte per seipsum non habet tantum virtutem collativam, ut ex principiis posset conclusiones deducere. Et ideo dicitur in I Post. [II⁴ (71b 17)], quod « demonstratio est syllogismus faciens scire ». Et per hunc modum ille qui demonstrat, auditorem scientem facit.

(2) This order of principles to conclusions is what St. Thomas calls the order of discipline. Cf. the prologue to the *Summa*. See also M.-D. CHENU, O.P., *Introduction à l'étude de Saint Thomas d'Aquin*. Montréal-Paris, 1950, pp. 258-265

in this way one who demonstrates a proposition causes his listener to understand it.

The formal nature of doctrine receives its clearest and briefest statement in the commentaries on Aristotle. In the *Commentary on the Metaphysics* [1] doctrine is defined as the generation of science. Here the word doctrine is used with reference to the speculative sciences which come into being by way of *propter quid* demonstration. A little farther on in the same text [2] the term is used with reference to the generation of those sciences which are not *propter quid* but *quia*.

In the *Commentary on the Physics* [3] *doctrina* is again defined as the generation of science. *Doctrina* is related to science as generation is related to that which is generated.

In one text we find the term *doctrina* used in the sense of *disciplina*. However, St. Thomas seems to be aware of this unusual use of the term, and qualifies it by saying *doctrina addiscentis* [4].

... Et dicit quod non sequitur, etiam si doctio et doctrina addiscentis essent idem, quod docere et addiscere essent idem; quia doctio et doctrina dicuntur in abstracto, docere autem et discere in concreto. Unde applicantur ad fines vel ad terminos, secundum quos sumitur diversa ratio actionis et passionis. ...

... Et dicit quod finaliter dicendum est, quod non sequitur quod actio et passio sunt idem, vel doctio vel doctrina, sed quod motus cui inest utrumque eorum, sit idem. Qui quidem motus secundum unam rationem est actio, et secundum aliam rationem est passio. ...

Looking into the Greek text of Aristotle we can understand why St. Thomas felt it necessary to qualify *doctrina* as *doctrina addiscentis*, because Aristotle had used the word μάθησις which is properly translated *disciplina*. St. Thomas, however, following the text of the translation he had at hand, uses the word *doctrina*, indicating by the qualification *addiscentis* that he means *disciplina*. The term *doctio* is used for *doctrina*.

(1) *In Metaph.*, VII, lect. 17 (ed. Cathala, 1670): « Et propter hoc de eis [substantiis simplicibus] etiam non potest esse doctrina, sicut est in scientiis speculativis. Nam doctrina est generatio scientiae; scientia autem fit in nobis per hoc quod scimus propter quid. Syllogismi enim demonstrativi facientis scire, medium est propter quid ».

(2) *Ibid.* (ed. Cathala, 1671).

(3) *In V Phys.*, cap. 2, lect. 3 (ed. Leon., II, p. 239): « ... Sicut se habet genus ad genus, sic et species ad speciem; si igitur generationis sit generatio, oportebit quod etiam doctrinae generatio sit doctrina. Sed hoc apparet manifeste falsum: doctrina enim est generatio scientiae, et non generatio doctrinae ».

(4) *In III Phys*, cap. 3, lect. 5 (ed. Leon. II, p. 113).

What is of particular importance for us in this text is that *doctrina* and *disciplina* are here used as illustrations of action and passion. Action and passion are not identical. Neither are *doctrina* and *disciplina*. Yet the movement *(motus)* in which action and passion exist is one and the same movement [1]. So too the movement in which *doctrina* and *disciplina* exist is one and the same. The movement is a movement of reason. Hence we may conclude that just as the same movement according to one aspect, i. e. *ut est ab agente,* is action, and according to another aspect, i. e. *ut est in passo,* is passion; so the same movement of reason according to one aspect, i. e. *ut est a docente,* is *doctrina,* and according to another aspect, i. e. *ut est in discipulo,* is *disciplina.*

The following text in which learning *(addiscere)* is spoken of as the generation of science in its passive aspect is another clear indication of the identity of the rational movement of teaching and discipline [2].

... Addiscere enim proprie est scientiam in aliquo generari. Quod autem generatur neque fuit omnino non ens neque omnino ens; sed quodammodo ens et quodammodo non ens: ens quidem in potentia, non ens vero actu: et hoc est generari, reduci de potentia in actum. Unde nec id quod quis addiscit erat omnino prius notum, ut Plato posuit, nec omnino ignotum, ut secundum solutionem supra improbatam ponebatur; sed erat notum potentia sive virtute in principiis praecognitis universalibus, ignotum autem actu, secundum propriam cognitionem. Et hoc est addiscere, reduci de cognitione potentiali, seu virtuali, aut universali, in cognitionem propriam et actualem.

We may well wonder why it is that St. Thomas has the tendency to speak of *doctrina* as the generation of science rather than the generation of any knowledge. He not only uses the term to refer to the acquisition of science but also recognizes the legitimacy of using this term to refer to the acquisition of any knowledge, even such knowledge as the rhetorician imparts and such as is received on faith.

One can see perhaps some analogy between the treatment of *doctrina* here and the treatment of science in Aristotle and St. Thomas. Science is the knowledge of conclusions through their principles. In its perfection science is knowledge through principles

(1) Cf. e. g. *S. T.* I, 42, 2c. Also Bernard Lonergan's article, « St. Thomas' Theory of Operation », *Theological Studies,* III (1942), pp. 375-402, esp. pp. 377-381.
(2) *In I Post. Anal.,* cap. 1, lect. 3 (ed. Leon, I, p. 148).

which cause the thing known to be and to be such as well as to be true; for the principles of being are the principles of truth. However, the notion of science is also verified in those knowledges which are called subalternate sciences and those which are *scientiae quia*, but in an imperfect manner. Nevertheless they merit to bear the name science, imperfectly however but not improperly; just as finite reality merits to bear the name being imperfectly but not improperly. Other knowledges, however, bear the name science only improperly; for example, the knowledge of first complex principles or the knowledge of history can be called science improperly.

In the treatment of science that which is perfect human science receives primary consideration; moreover, in giving the definition of science we define perfect human science. For example, we find the brief definitions *scientia est cognitio per causas* and *scire est cognoscere propter quid* scattered all through the works of St. Thomas and Aristotle.

Now it seems we have something similar in the case of St. Thomas' treatment of human doctrine. In its perfection human doctrine is the generation of science by way of verbal discourse. However, the notion of doctrine is verified imperfectly in the generation of any new knowledge in the disciple from knowledge previously possessed. Thus the teaching of the rhetorician as well as the teaching of truths to be accepted on faith may be properly called doctrine, although imperfectly; imperfect in so far as it does not generate new knowledge with necessity but dependent on the free will of the disciple. In the case of generating knowledges whose object is immediately evident, such as the first complex principles, the generation of such knowledge is doctrine purely and solely *per accidens*, since such activity is not the proper function of the teacher, and hence we may say that it is improperly called doctrine.

What is essential to the notion of human doctrine as expounded by St. Thomas is the discourse of reason which is induced in the disciple by the teacher functioning as a cause of the new knowledge acquired by the disciple and this discourse has its principle in pre-existing knowledge and its term in new knowledge acquired.

The reason why the teaching of the first complex principles would not properly be called doctrine is not because in this case there is no rational discourse in the disciple terminating in new knowledge. For even in this case there is some discourse, in so far as all truths, even those most primary in human knowledge, are known by the intellect composing subject with predicate. The reason would rather be that the teacher in this case is not a cause *per se* of this knowledge: whereas in the case of truths received on faith from a teacher, there is a rational discourse induced in the disciple and the teacher is a cause *per se* of the knowledge acquired.

The rational discourse, in which doctrine consists, will differ according to the kind of knowledge communicated. When scientific knowledge is the object of doctrine, the process will be demonstration *propter quid* or *quia*, depending on the perfection of the science in question. When knowledge which is the object of rhetorical doctrine is communicated, the enthymeme or some such process will be used. When knowledge which is to be received on faith is communicated, the concepts of subject and predicate will be presented and then affirmed or denied by the intellect composing and dividing through the external medium of authority, although here too a presentation of the reasonableness or moral necessity of making the affirmation or negation may be given.

Doctrine, therefore, as it exists, is not of one kind, one species. It is of several species, even of several genera. For doctrine is not a proximate genus any more than science; there are several genera of science as well as several species.

To understand this we may consider that the unity of any movement is caused by the unity of its term, but the difference or diversity of movement is caused by the difference or diversity of principle. The reason, for example, why two lines terminating at the same point are different is that they have different principles. Difference of terms in movement is the first indication of difference of movement; but even if two movements terminate at the same term, the movements are different if their principles are different [1].

We can say, therefore, that doctrines as movements of reason will be different or diverse if they have different or diverse principles. The action or rational movement signified by the word doctrine is signified, therefore, as being under a certain indetermination. Now signifying the whole actuality according to its de-

(1) Cf. *In I Post. Anal.*, cap. 28, lect. 41 (ed. Leon., I, pp. 305-307). This text will come up for consideration again later. See pages 106-108.

74

terminable part is the function of the concept as it stands under the intention of genus. Doctrine, however, as it exists, is always of a determined kind.

I think we have now sufficiently determined the nature of human doctrine according to St. Thomas. We have gone beyond the text of St. Thomas only in attempting to explain why he seems to prefer to speak of doctrine as the generation of science rather than of any knowledge and in indicating how doctrine is generic in its signification.

St. Thomas uses the term, however, not only in its formal sense, but also in several other senses. We have seen some texts in which the term may be understood as signifying the verbal discourse of a teacher[1]. In such expressions also as *ut patet per doctrinam Dionysii in libro ' de Div. Nom. '*[2], the term *doctrina* may have this meaning. For this meaning is indicated in parallel expressions, such as for example, *quod expresse dictis Dionysii... contrariari videtur*[3]. Likewise in the expressions *qui falsam doctrinam enuntiant* and *qui veram doctrinam enuntiant*[4] the term *doctrina* signifies the verbal discourse, the propositions enuntiated by one who is teaching.

However, in such expressions as *secundum doctrinam Domini*[5], *secundum doctrinam Aristotelis*[6], etc., *doctrina* very probably signifies *id quod docetur*, the object of doctrine, its final cause; for the substitution *secundum id quod docetur a Domino*, for example, seems to express exactly the sense of *secundum doctrinam Domini*.

Doctrina in this objective or final sense can be considered from two points of view. The knowledge generated by doctrine can be regarded either as a body of knowledge (a body of conclusions when the object of doctrine is science), or as the habit of this knowledge. Thus *doctrina* can have a twofold objective sense.

Hence if *doctrina* is understood in its objective sense in the expression *doctrina philosophica*, this expression may mean either a body of philosophical knowledge which is taught, or the habit of this knowledge. Although I have not found any instance in which St. Thomas can certainly be said to use *doctrina* to signify

(1) See above, pages 64-65.
(2) *S. T.*, I, 75, 5, ob. 1.
(3) *In II Sent.*, d. 9, q. 1, a. 2, ad 4.
(4) *S. T.*, II-II, 178, 2, ad 3.
(5) *S. T.*, II-II, 187, 6, ad 3.
(6) *Ver.*, 11, 1c.

the habit of a knowledge generated by doctrine, nevertheless this meaning of doctrine should be recognized as one of the possible meanings of the term. At least we shall allow for it in our consideration of the meaning of *sacra doctrina* especially since some of the commentators accept this sense of the term.

In summary, then, we may say that *doctrina* is the generation of knowledge. It can take place in two ways: 1) by way of illumination, i. e. affording the intellectual light in which the object is seen; God and angels teach in this way; 2) by way of speech, i. e. by presenting the object to be known; God, angels, and men can teach in this way. Moreover, we may recognize six meanings of the term *doctrina* in St. Thomas: 1) the generation of science (or any knowledge not habitually possessed) by way of illumination; 2) the generation of science (or any knowledge not habitually possessed) by way of speech; 3) the verbal discourse by means of which this knowledge is generated; 4) the knowledge or science which is generated, *id quod docetur;* doctrine in the sense of its object, its final cause, considered as a body of knowledge or a body of conclusions; 5) the habit of knowledge generated; 6) discipline, the reception of knowledge from another.

The first two meanings of the term are analogous by the analogy of proportionality. However, we shall not delay on this point.

The second, third, fourth, and fifth meanings are analogous by the analogy of attribution. For *doctrina* which is formally the rational discourse induced in the disciple has its cause in the verbal discourse of the teacher and its effect in the knowledge acquired by the disciple. When therefore *doctrina* is predicated of the verbal discourse of the teacher or of the knowledge acquired by the disciple, the term is used analogously by the analogy of attribution, such as is found when health is predicated of medicine and urine, though health is formally only in the body. Health is predicated of medicine in so far as medicine is the cause of health in the body. It is predicated of urine in so far as urine is the sign or effect of health in the body.

Likewise in the case of doctrine. Although doctrine is formally the rational discourse induced in the disciple, it is predicated of the verbal discourse of the teacher in so far as this is the cause of doctrine. It is predicated of the knowledge communicated in so far as this is the effect or final cause of doctrine, which can be considered either as a body of knowledge or a habit of knowledge.

76

This analogous use of terminology is common in St. Thomas. We find it frequently in his use of the terms *intellectus*, *scientia*, *sapientia*, etc., which are applied analogously to the habits, acts, and objects concerned. Science, for example, which we may regard as formally consisting in the habit of conclusions, is predicated also of the conclusions produced by the habit and even of their external expression, either oral or written. Moreover, it should not surprise us if St. Thomas uses the word science to signify doctrine in so far as doctrine is the cause of science, just as the word doctrine can be used to signify science, in so far as science is the effect of doctrine.

Now the word doctrine retains its generic signification in all of its analogous uses. It does not specify of itself the kind of doctrine involved. However, in a context where a certain qualification is indicated or understood, the term as modified by this qualification or context may signify doctrine which is scientific or doctrine which pertains to rhetoric, etc., depending on the qualification indicated or understood.

Here we find some similarity to the use of the word animal, which is used of men and brutes. In a given context, where some sort of specification is understood, e. g. irrational, the term with its context signifies brutes; as for example, in the sentence: The woods is populated with animals, the cities with men. However, in the sentence: some animals cook their food, the term animal as qualified by the context can refer only to rational animals.

With this background from St. Thomas' own discussion of the meaning of the word *doctrina* and his use of the term, and keeping in mind the lesson he has taught us of seeking the meaning of the word in its context, we can hope to investigate with profit the meaning of the term *sacra doctrina* in the first question of the *Summa*.

CHAPTER III

THE MEANING OF *SACRA DOCTRINA*
IN THE *SUMMA*

The Prologue

The prologue to the *Summa* gives us some insight into St. Thomas' use of the term *sacra doctrina*. St. Thomas here tells us the purpose of his *Summa Theologica*; namely, to present those truths which pertain to the Christian religion in a manner adapted to the instruction of beginners in this doctrine. To do this is part of his obligation as a doctor of Catholic truth.

It is his considered opinion that beginners in this doctrine are greatly hindered in their progress by what has been written by various authors: partly because of the multiplication of useless questions, articles, and arguments; partly too because what is necessary for such beginners to understand the matter is not presented according to the order of discipline; and partly because the frequent repetition of the same things causes weariness and confusion in the minds of the readers. Taking care to avoid these defects, he will attempt to carry out with brevity and clarity what pertains to sacred doctrine in so far as the matter will allow [1].

---

(1) *S. T.*, prol.: — Quia catholicae veritatis doctor non solum provectos debet instruere, sed ad eum pertinet etiam incipientes erudire, secundum illud Apostoli I *ad Cor.*, III[1]: « Tanquam parvulis in Christo, lac vobis potum dedi, non escam »; propositum nostrae intentionis in hoc opere est, ea quae ad Christianam religionem pertinet eo modo tradere secundum quod congruit ad eruditionem incipientium.

Consideravimus namque huius doctrinae novitios in his quae a diversis conscripta sunt plurimum impediri; partim quidem propter multiplicationem inutilium quaestionum, articulorum et argumentorum; partim etiam quia ea quae sunt necessaria talibus ad sciendum non traduntur secundum ordinem disciplinae, sed secundum quod requirebat librorum expositio, vel secundum quod se prae-

Here we meet St. Thomas, *the doctor catholicae veritatis,* explaining the *raison d'être* of his work. It is in function of his being a teacher of Catholic truth that he is undertaking the work of instructing beginners in those things which pertain to the Christian religion. What he is presenting is Catholic truth. Moreover, his work will be carried out in a manner adapted to the minds of those whom he is teaching.

We notice that St. Thomas considers his work from four points of view: that of the teacher, his disciples, the matter taught, and the manner of his teaching. These four considerations correspond to the four causes that contribute to the intelligibility of the formal notion of doctrine which we investigated in chapter two. This already may be some indication of St. Thomas' understanding of the term *sacra doctrina.*

In order to confine his effort within some certain limits, St. Thomas finds it necessary first to make an investigation of sacred doctrine itself in order to discover what sort of thing it is and what it includes. He divides this investigation into ten questions about sacred doctrine. The tenth question, however, will not be about sacred doctrine itself, but the Sacred Writing or Sacred Books of this doctrine. This already indicates some distinction to be made between sacred doctrine and Sacred Scripture [1].

The First Article

In the first article St. Thomas investigates the necessity of this doctrine. The objections presented try to show the superfluity of a

---

bebat occasio disputandi; partim quidem quia eorumdem frequens repetitio et fastidium et confusionem generabat in animis auditorum.

Haec igitur et alia huiusmodi evitare studentes, tentabimus, cum confidentia divini auxilii, ea quae ad sacram doctrina pertinent breviter ac dilucide prosequi, secundum quod materia patietur.

(1) *S. T.*, I, 1 introd.: — Et ut intentio nostra sub aliquibus certis limitibus comprehendatur, necessarium est primo investigare de ipsa sacra doctrina, qualis sit et ad quae se extendat.

Circa quae quaerenda decem.

Primo: de necessitate huius doctrinae.
Secundo: utrum sit scientia.
Tertio: utrum sit una vel plures.
Quarto: utrum sit speculativa vel practica.
Quinto: de comparatione eius ad alias scientias.
Sexto: utrum sit sapientia.
Septimo: quid sit subiectum eius.
Octavo: utrum sit argumentativa.
Nono: utrum uti debeat metaphoricis vel symbolicis locutionibus.
Decimo: utrum Scriptura Sacra huius doctrinae sit secundum plures sensus exponenda.

doctrine distinct from the philosophical disciplines. In the response St. Thomas shows the necessity of some doctrine according to divine revelation which is distinct from the philosophical disciplines, and further specifies this doctrine as sacred doctrine.

He shows that this doctrine is necessary because man must possess the knowledge of certain truths in order to achieve salvation. The truths which concern man's supernatural end are beyond the comprehension of reason. However, he must know these truths in order to direct his actions to that end. Hence it is necessary that certain truths be made known to him by way of revelation.

Moreover, even in regard to those truths about God which are not beyond the comprehension of reason, it was necessary that man be instructed by divine revelation. For few men attain the knowledge of this kind of truth about God, and then only after a long time and with an admixture of many errors. And yet on this kind of truth about God, which can be known through reason, depends the entire salvation of man. Hence in order that the salvation of men come about in a more fitting and more certain manner, it was necessary that men be instructed in divine things through divine revelation.

Therefore besides the philosophical disciplines which carry on their investigations by way of human reason, another doctrine was necessary, namely sacred doctrine which proceeds by way of revelation [1].

We should note well that St. Thomas is not demonstrating the necessity of a knowledge of divine truths for salvation. That is one of his premises. He argues from this necessity of a knowledge

---

(1) *S. T.*, I, 1, 1c: — Respondeo. Dicendum quod necessarium fuit ad humanam salutem esse doctrinam quandam secundum revelationem divinam praeter philosophicas disciplinas, quae ratione humana investigantur. Primo quidem quia homo ordinatur ad Deum sicut ad quendam finem qui comprehensionem rationis excedit, secundum illud *Isaiae* LXIV[4]: « Oculus non vidit Deus absque te, quae praeparasti diligentibus te ». Finem autem oportet esse praecognitum hominibus, qui suas intentiones et actiones debent ordinare ad finem. Unde necessarium fuit homini ad salutem quod ei nota fierent quaedam per revelationem divinam, quae rationem humanam excedunt.

Ad ea etiam quae de Deo ratione humana investigari possunt, necessarium fuit hominem instrui revelatione divina. Quia veritas de Deo per rationem investigata, a paucis, et per longum tempus, et cum admixtione multoru m errorum homini proveniret; a cuius tamen veritatis cognitione dependet tota hominis salus, quae in Deo est. Ut igitur salus hominibus et convenientius et certius proveniat, necessarium fuit quod de divinis per divinam revelationem instruantur.

Necessarium igitur fuit praeter philosophicas doctrinas, quae per rationem investigantur, sacram doctrinam per revelationem haberi.

of divine truths to the necessity of *their being made known* through revelation, since it is either physically or morally impossible for all men to know them except by being instructed in them through revelation.

The conclusion therefore is the necessity of some instruction in divine things through revelation. This instruction in divine things is called *sacra doctrina*.

This is clear from a comparison of the conclusions of the various parts of the article:

... necessarium fuit...
1 quod *ei nota fierent* quaedam per revelationem divinam
2 quod de divinis per divinam revelationem *instruantur*
3 *sacram doctrinam* per revelationem haberi.

In the first two instances that which is necessary is expressed by verbs (*notum facere, instruere*) which signify an action. Men must receive this action; they must be instructed. In the final conclusion this action is expressed by the term *sacra doctrina*. *Sacra doctrina* then must signify this action of making known, of instructing men in divine things.

St. Thomas has told us before that doctrine takes place by way of speech: *doctrina fit per locutionem.* Now he tells us that sacred doctrine takes place by way of divine speech: *sacram doctrinam per revelationem haberi.*

Revelation, as St. Thomas conceives it, is a kind of hierarchical operation [1]. Supernatural truth comes to men like the waters of a stream falling in cascades from heaven to earth; from God, its source, to the angels in their hierarchies, and from angels to men. From the Prophets and Apostles, the first to drink of this stream, it flows down the centuries, and through the perennial *magisterium* of Christ's Church, its Fathers, Doctors, teachers, missionaries, and catechists, it comes to all men whose reason is disposed by faith to drink of these waters.

Revelation in its perfection is found in heaven where God reveals His Eternal Word directly and immediately to the angels and the blessed [2]. This revelation, however, has many participated

(1) Cf. E. GILSON, *Le Thomisme.*[5] Paris: J. Vrin, 1947, p. 21.
(2) *S. T.*, II-II, 171, 4, ad 2: — Ad Secundum. Dicendum quod prophetia est sicut quiddam imperfectum in genere divinae revelationis; unde dicitur I *ad Cor.*, XIII[8], « quod prophetiae evacuabuntur, et quod ex parte prophetamus »,

forms. The revelation to the prophets is but one of its participations, something imperfect in the genus of revelation. Sacred Scripture is still another more imperfect image of the Word spoken by God to the blessed. Revelation, moreover, continues to be participated in still lower forms in the words of the Fathers, Doctors, teachers, preachers, and missionaries of the Church, who bring to all men in each succeeding age the ever same truth revealed by God to His prophets and apostles [1]. Thus God continues His revelation down through the centuries through the instrumentality of the Mystical Body of His Son.

The deposit of truth which is brought to men through the ministrations of God's Church was, of course, closed with the death of the last Apostle. But this same truth continues to be made known and to be unfolded not only through the infallible pronouncements of the Vicar of Christ and in the infallible teachings of its Ordinary Magistracy but also in the discourses, sermons, and writings of its competent members and under its scrutinizing, infallible eye.

Thus sacred doctrine, the instruction of men in divine truth, is carried on through revelation. It is not identical with revelation; rather revelation is the means by which sacred doctrine is carried on.

Moreover, sacred doctrine denotes the instruction carried on by God through the ministers of His Word in so far as this instruction proceeds under the influence of the infused light of faith. For St. Thomas does not use the term *sacra doctrina* with reference to the communication of God's knowledge under the light of glory or the light of prophecy or any other supernatural light, although he speaks of the communication of God's knowledge in the light of glory as *doctrina* [2].

idest imperfecte. Perfectio autem divinae revelationis erit in patria, unde subditur [10]: « Cum venerit quod perfectum est, evacuabitur quod ex parte est ». Unde non oportet quod propheticae revelationi nihil desit, sed quod nihil desit eorum ad quae prophetia ordinatur.

(1) *S. T.*, II-II, 2, 6c : — Respondeo. Dicendum quod explicatio credendorum fit per revelationem divinam : credibilia enim naturalem rationem excedunt. Revelatio autem divina ordine quodam ad inferiores pervenit per superiores ; sicut ad homines per angelos, et ad inferiores angelos per superiores, ut patet per Dionysium in *De Cael. Hier.* Et ideo a pari ratione explicatio fidei oportet quod perveniat ad inferiores homines per maiores. Et ideo sicut superiores angeli, qui inferiores illuminant, habent pleniorem notitiam de rebus divinis quam inferiores, ut dicit Dionysius, XII cap. *De Cael. Hier.*: ita etiam superiores homines, ad quos pertinet alios erudire, tenentur habere pleniorem notitiam de credendis et magis explicite credere.

(2) Cf. *Ver.* 11, 4, ad 1.

St. Thomas tells us that this divine instruction carried on under the influence of the light of faith accompishes its results in a gradual, successive manner. For although man has been given a participation of divine goodness by reason of which his ultimate beatitude consists in a certain supernatural vision of God, this gift did not change the manner of his acquisition of knowledge. Man cannot attain the vision of God except by way of being a disciple learning from God his teacher, according to the words of St. John: « Omnis, qui audivit a Patre, et didicit, venit ad me ». However, he partakes of this discipline, not all at once, but gradually, according to the condition of his nature. Every disciple of this kind must first believe in order to arrive at perfect knowledge, as even Aristotle says that one who is learning must believe. Hence in order that man arrive at the perfect vision of beatitude, it is required that he first believe God as a disciple believes his master [1].

St. Thomas further explains why this instruction first terminates in faith on the part of the disciple [2]. The reason for this is that

(1) *S. T.*, II-II, 2, 3c: — ... perfectio ergo rationalis creaturae non solum consistit in eo, quod ei attribuitur secundum suam naturam, sed in eo etiam, quod ei attribuitur ex quadam supernaturali participatione divinae bonitatis; unde et supra dictum est [I-II, 3, 8], quod ultima beatitudo hominis consistit, in quadam supernaturali Dei visione: ad quam homo pertingere non potest, nisi per modum addiscentis a Deo doctore, secundum illud *Joan.*, VI, 45: « Omnis, qui audit a Patre et didicit venit ad me ». Huius autem disciplinae fit homo particeps non statim, sed successive, secundum modum suae naturae. Omnis autem talis addiscens oportet quod credat, ad hoc quod ad perfectam scientiam perveniat, sicut etiam Philosophus dicit quod « oportet addiscentem credere ». Unde ad hoc quod homo perveniat ad perfectam visionem beatitudinis praeexigitur quod credat Deo tamquam discipulus magistro docenti.

(2) *Ver.*, 14, 10c: — Respondeo. Dicendum, quod habere fidem de his quae sunt supra rationem, necessarium est ad vitam aeternam consequendam.

Quod hinc accipi potest. Non enim contingit aliquid de imperfecto ad perfectum adduci nisi per actionem alicuius perfecti. Nec perfecti actio ab imperfecto statim recipitur in principio perfecte; sed primo quidem imperfecte postea perfecte, et sic deinde quousque ad perfectionem perveniat. Et hoc quidem manifestum est in omnibus rebus naturalibus quae per successionem temporis aliquam perfectionem consequuntur. Et similiter videmus in operibus humanis, et praecipue in disciplinis.

In principio enim homo imperfectus est in cognitione. Ad hoc autem quod perfectionem scientiae consequatur, indiget aliquo instruente, qui eum ad perfectionem scientiae ducat; quod facere non posset, nisi ipse perfecte scientiam haberet, utpote comprehendens rationes eorum quae sub scientiam cadunt. Non autem in principio suae doctrinae statim ei qui instruitur, tradit rationes subtilium de quibus instruere intendit; quia tunc statim in principio scientiam haberet perfecte qui instruitur; sed tradit ei quaedam, quorum rationes tunc, cum primo instruitur discipulus, nescit; sciet autem postea perfectus in scientia.

Et ideo dicitur, quod oportet addiscentem credere: et aliter ad perfectam scientiam pervenire non posset, nisi scilicet supponeret ea quae sibi in principio traduntur, quorum rationes tunc capere non potest.

Ultima autem perfectio ad quam homo ordinatur, consistit in perfecta Dei

no subject is reduced from the state of imperfection to perfection except through the action of a perfect agent. But this action is not at once perfectly received by an imperfect subject in the beginning. First it is received imperfectly, and afterwards perfectly, and so finally the subject arrives at perfection. This can be seen in all natural things which acquire some perfection gradually in the course of time. Likewise we see it in all human accomplishment, and especially in disciplines.

For in the beginning man is imperfect in knowledge. To arrive at the perfection of science he needs some teacher who will instruct him and lead him to the perfection of science. This the teacher could not do, unless he himself possessed the science in its perfection, comprehending the reasons for the truths that come under his science. In the beginning of his doctrine, however, he does not immediately give his disciple the reasons for subtle truths which he is going to teach, because then already in the beginning the disciple would know the science perfectly. Rather he presents some truths for which the disciple does not know the reasons, when he is first being instructed. He will know them later when he has acquired the science perfectly.

And so it is necessary for one who is learning to believe. For he would not otherwise be able to arrive at the perfection of science, unless he believed in the beginning the truths presented; he could not at that time understand the reasons for them.

Now the ultimate perfection to which man is ordered consists in the perfect knowledge of God. Man cannot attain this knowledge except by the operation and instruction of God Who has a perfect knowledge of Himself. However, owing to the principles of his knowledge, man is not immediately capable of a perfect knowledge of God. He must receive it by way of receiving some truths on

cognitione: ad quam quidem pervenire non potest nisi operatione et instructione Dei, qui est sui perfectus cognitor. Perfectae autem cognitionis statim homo in sui principio capax non est; unde oportet quod accipiat per viam credendi aliqua, per quae manuducatur ad perveniendum in perfectam cognitionem.

Quorum *quaedam* talia sunt, quod in hac vita de eis perfecta cognitio haberi non potest, quae totaliter vim humanae rationis excedunt: et ista oportet credere quamdiu in statu viae sumus; videbimus autem ea perfecte in statu patriae. *Quaedam* vero sunt ad quae etiam in hac vita perfecte cognoscenda possumus pervenire sicut illa quae de Deo demonstrative probari possunt; quae tamen a principio necesse est credere, propter quinque rationes, quas Rabbi Moyses ponit.

(The five reasons which follow are suggested in summary fashion by St. Thomas in the first article of the *Summa*).

faith, and through them he is led by the hand, as it were, to the goal of perfect knowledge.

Some of these truths are such that it is impossible for man in this life to know them perfectly; they entirely exceed the power of human reason. These we must believe so long as we are on earth, but we shall know them perfectly in heaven.

Others, however, are such that we can know them perfectly in this life; for example, those truths about God which can be demonstrated. Yet in the beginning we must believe even these.

Still other truths can be deduced from those truths which we must believe so long as we are on earth. And these also the disciple can be led to understand (*scire*). And although this knowledge is imperfect in so far as its principles are not self-evident, nevertheless it truly merits to bear the name science in so far as it is a knowledge of conclusions which are seen to follow from principles and is in continuity with God's own knowledge through principles accepted on faith [1].

The ultimate term of this doctrine is the contemplation of divine truth itself in heaven, where the imperfection of our knowledge will be resolved in the perfect knowledge which God has of Himself [2]. The proportioned end of this doctrine is the contemplation of divine truth through reason enlightened by faith [3]. And so sacred doctrine finds its proportioned term in the habit of supernatural wisdom acquired, a wisdom which is science *par excellence* [4].

Hence this instruction begins in imparting knowledge which is accepted on faith, leads on to science and wisdom, and has its ultimate term and resolution in the vision of God Himse f.

(1) *Ver.*, 14, 9, ad 3. — Ad Tertium dicendum, quod ille qui habet scientiam subalternatam, non perfecte attingit ad rationem sciendi, nisi in quantum eius cognitio continuatur quodammodo cum cognitione eius qui habet scientiam subalternantem. Nihilominus tamen inferior sciens non dicitur de his quae supponit, habere scientiam, sed de conclusionibus, quae ex principiis suppositis de necessitate concluduntur. Et sic fidelis potest dici habere scientiam de his quae concluduntur ex articulis fidei.

Cf. also M.-D. CHENU, O.P., *La théologie comme science* ..., pp. 78-79.

(2) *In I Sent.*, prol., q. 1, a. 3, sol. I.

(3) *Ibid.*, sol. III: — ... ratio manuducta per fidem excrescit in hoc ut ipsa credibilia plenius comprehendat, et tunc ipsa quodammodo intelligit: unde dicitur Isa., VII, secundum aliam litteram: *Nisi credideritis, non intelligetis.*

(4) *S. T.*, I-II, 57, 2, ad 1: — Ad primum. Dicendum quod sapientia est quaedam scientia, inquantum habet id quod est commune omnibus scientiis, ut scilicet ex principiis conclusiones demonstret. Sed quia habet aliquid proprium supra alias scientias, inquantum scilicet de omnibus iudicat, et non solum quantum ad conclusiones, sed etiam quantum ad prima principia, ideo habet rationem perfectioris virtutis quam scientia.

Thus St. Thomas explains the instruction in divine truth by way of revelation. This is the instruction which he calls sacred doctrine. It is an action to which man is subject, and to which he must submit himself in order to be saved. Using St. Thomas' own words we can define it as instruction in divine things by way of revelation.

Now if we compare this article of the *Summa* with its companion article in the *Commentary*, we shall see that St. Thomas' use of the term in the *Summa* indicates a definite advance in the appreciation of its meaning. In the *Commentary*, *sacra doctrina* is described as the doctrine which proceeds from the principles of faith, which leads to the contemplation of God through the inspired knowledge of faith as medium, which considers reality *secundum rationes ex inspiratione divini luminis acceptas* [1]. There is question explicitly only of the necessity of some doctrine beginning with a knowledge of faith and leading to the contemplation of God; i. e. proceeding from explicit faith to science and wisdom. The argument for its necessity, like the argument in the *Summa,* is based on the necessary proportion between means and end. But in the *Commentary* St. Thomas is speaking only of sacred doctrine in the advanced phase of its reception; and this he calls *doctrina theologiae*. For sacred doctrine even in its advanced phase is necessary if man is to advance in knowledge which is proportioned to his end. But still even though it terminates merely in faith, it is sufficient for those who are unable to receive this action more perfectly. Hence, St. Thomas does not say that *doctrina theologiae* is necessary for salvation.

In the *Summa,* however, there is question of the necessity of *sacra doctrina* for salvation. This instruction, being an action which is not received in the recipient perfectly in the beginning, first terminates in faith. Only with the progress of doctrine will the disciple be moved to science and wisdom. Regardless of whether this doctrine is to be received with greater or less perfection, man must submit himself to this action if he is to have the knowledge necessary for directing himself to his supernatural end.

Unless St. Thomas had understood the term *sacra doctrina* as an action which can be more or less perfectly received, he would never have been able to use it as he does in the first article of

(1) *In I Sent.*, prol., q. 1, a. 1, ad 1. Cf. above, pp. 45-47.

the *Summa,* where he considers the necessity of instruction in divine things which terminates merely in faith in the first phase of its reception, whereas in the later phase it terminates in science and wisdom, imperfect as it may be.

Now let us consider the objections and their answers in the first article of the *Summa.* We have examined the first objection and response before [1]. Here St. Thomas says that sacred doctrine consists in that kind of truth which is revealed by God and which we must believe. We saw that he could not be *identifying* sacred doctrine with this kind of truth, but that sacred doctrine must be said to consist in this kind of truth as in its origin, in its roots, in its principle. Here, however, we must add the observation that St. Thomas is not speaking of our knowledge of this truth, but of this truth which exists independently of our knowledge of it, truth which is God's own knowledge, which is revealed, and which we must believe. In this truth sacred doctrine has its origin, its roots, its principle, just as the truth known by any teacher is the source and principle of his instruction. Moreover, in so far as this truth is believed by man it serves as the principles by which the action of sacred doctrine progresses from faith to science and wisdom. And finally, as this instruction terminates in the contemplation of this truth, sacred doctrine must be said to consist in this truth as in its end, *finaliter.*

Thus we have a fuller understanding of the simple statement with which St. Thomas concludes this response: ... *et in huiusmodi sacra doctrina consistit.*

Moreover, St. Thomas has thus reinforced his demonstration of the necessity of sacred doctrine, since sacred doctrine in its origin, principle, and end is concerned with a kind of truth which is necessary for man to know, but which is not accessible to him through any human discipline.

The response to the second objection has been a source of difficulty for all commentators on the term *sacra doctrina.* Some have thought that St. Thomas here identifies sacred doctrine with the science of sacred theology, and hence is using the term in a meaning different from that found in the body of the article. Up to his response St. Thomas has said nothing explicitly about sacred doctrine in its role as science. But now he is forced to indicate

(1) Cf. above, pp. 39-44.

the manner in which sciences are distinguished in order to answer an objection. The objection is stated as follows[1]: A doctrine can be only about being. But all beings are considered in the philosophical disciplines, even God; hence a certain part of philosophy is called theology, or divine science. Hence there is no necessity for another doctrine besides the philosophical disciplines.

The answer to this objection begins by stating the principle that a diverse reason of cognoscibility causes diversity in science. This principle is then illustrated by an example: — even though the astrologer and natural philosopher demonstrate the same conclusion, their sciences are diverse, because they make use of diverse *media* of cognoscibility in their demonstrations. Hence, St. Thomas concludes, nothing prevents the same things which are treated in the philosophical disciplines in so far as they are cognoscible by the light of human reason from being treated in another science in so far as they are cognoscible by the light of divine revelation. Therefore, St. Thomas finally concludes, the theology which pertains to sacred doctrine differs generically from that theology which is set down as part of philosophy.

In this response we must consider three things. First, St. Thomas refuses to identify sacred doctrine with the science of theology. He tells us only that theology pertains to sacred doctrine and is generically different from the theology which is part of philosophy. If he is here speaking of the habit of sacred theology, then theology pertains to sacred doctrine, the instruction in divine things by way of revelation, as its final term or effect in the disciple. Thus in proving that the science which this instruction imparts is generically different from the science imparted in the philosophical

(1) *S. T.* I, 1, 1, ad 2: — Praeterea. Doctrina non potest esse nisi de ente; nihil enim scitur nisi verum, quod cum ente convertitur. Sed de omnibus entibus tractatur in philosophicis disciplinis, et etiam de Deo; unde quaedam pars philosophiae dicitur theologia, sive scientia divina, ut patet per Philosophum in VI *Metaph.* Non fuit igitur necessarium praeter philosophicas disciplinas aliam doctrinam haberi.
. . . . .
Ad Secundum. Dicendum quod diversa ratio cognoscibilis diversitatem scientiarum inducit. Eandem enim conclusionem demonstrat astrologus et naturalis, puta quod terra est rotunda; sed astrologus per medium mathematicum, idest a materia abstractum; naturalis autem per medium circa materiam consideratum. Unde nihil prohibet de eisdem rebus, de quibus philosophicae disciplinae tractant secundum quod sunt cognoscibilia lumine naturalis rationis, et aliam scientiam tractare secundum quod cognoscuntur lumine divinae revelationis. Unde theologia quae ad sacram doctrinam pertinet, differt secundum genus ab illa theologia quae pars philosophiae ponitur.

disciplines, St. Thomas clearly answers the objection against the necessity of sacred doctrine.

Secondly, St. Thomas here goes to the ultimate root of the diversity between the philosophical sciences and theology, using the term *ratio cognoscibilis* which is eminently suited to his purpose. One reason for this, of course, is that since the philosophical sciences themselves are generically different within the higher genus of natural human knowledge, he must ascend to the reason for the diversity between natural and supernatural knowledge. But he does this also for another reason. In this article he is speaking of an action carried on through revelation and under the light of revelation. The knowledge imparted by this action is of two kinds, faith and theology, depending on the degree in which this action is received in the intellect. Faith is a knowledge caused directly by the light of divine revelation; theology, indirectly by this light as reflected in the crystal of human reasoning. In resorting to the ultimate source of diversity between natural and supernatural knowledge, St. Thomas is distinguishing the whole field of natural knowledges from the knowledges imparted by sacred doctrine. However, since the objection is presented in terms of knowledge which is science, St. Thomas is content merely to conclude that the theology which sacred doctrine imparts is generically different from the theology which is part of philosophy.

Thirdly, the terms *doctrina, disciplina,* and *scientia* can thus be understood in this response and throughout the article in their formal sense. Doctrine and discipline signify the rational operation of acquiring knowledge. Doctrine signifies this operation as induced by the teacher, discipline as received in the disciple. The knowledge acquired by the philosophical disciplines is science, that acquired by sacred doctrine is faith as well as science. Moreover, St. Thomas' preference for the term sacred doctrine over the term sacred discipline can be explained by the fact that this operation is sacred because it proceeds from God as our teacher through revelation, not because it is received by us. Whereas since human doctrine carries no reference to a particular teacher, the operation it signifies can more suitably be referred to with its reference to the disciple, i. e. as a discipline. Thus we can see how exceptionally well St. Thomas poses the question in this article: ... *Videtur quod non sit necessarium praeter philosophicas disciplinas aliam doctrinam haberi.*

Hence throughout this first article sacred doctrine may very well retain the same sense, namely instruction in divine things by way of revelation. Moreover, the science of sacred theology pertains to this instruction, and therefore this instruction is in some sense science. In what sense? This is the question St. Thomas answers in the next article.

The Second Article

In article two of the first question St. Thomas discusses whether sacred doctrine is science. As we have pointed out in the first chapter there is considerable difference of opinion among commentators on the meaning of *sacra doctrina* in this second article. Cajetan has given us one method of approach in determining the meaning of the subject term *sacra doctrina*. Fr. Bonnefoy has suggested to us another method of approach in determining the meaning of the predicate term *scientia*. The principle used by Cajetan is: *talia sunt subjecta qualia permittuntur a praedicatis.* That suggested to us by Fr. Bonnefoy's procedure is: *talia sunt praedicata qualia permittuntur a subjectis.* We have not denied the validity of either principle.

However, in the application of either of these principles great caution is needed in this case especially because up to the present neither the meaning of the subject term nor of the predicate term has been determined with certainty. Fr. Bonnefoy was well aware of the caution needed in this regard and his procedure is laudable, though mingled with mistakes of interpretation. From the definition of *sacra doctrina* which he finds in the first article and sees confirmed all through the first question by reason of texts which seem to identify *sacra doctrina* with *Sacra Scriptura,* he can proceed in the second article to the conclusion that since St. Thomas cannot be accused of beginning to treat one subject in a question and straightway change the subject he is considering, the term science predicated of this subject can be understood only as *scientia improprie dicta: talia sunt praedicata qualia permittuntur a subjectis.*

But Fr. Bonnefoy does not rest content with this so-called *a priori* conclusion. The main burden of his work consists in verifying the results suggested by this approach to the problem. This is done at some length and with considerable skill by assembling various texts from St. Thomas which conduct him to the conclusion that a science which has the articles of faith as its principles and the certitude of faith in its conclusions can be called science only improperly.

My objective here is to discover the meaning of the subject term *sacra doctrina* in the second article of the *Summa*. Both the principle of Cajetan and that of Fr. Bonnefoy will prove useful, as both subject and predicate terms are frequently used analogously by St. Thomas. In regard to the predicate term it will be sufficient for my purpose to inquire whether it is here understood as a habit of science, or conclusions known in virtue of their principles, or the generation of conclusions terminating finally in the habit acquired. In regard to the subject term, by reason of its meaning in article one, it can suggest an interpretation of the predicate which, however, must be checked in the context to see whether it is valid or not.

If our analysis of the first article is correct, the meaning of *sacra doctrina* as used there is the instruction in divine things by way of revelation; or more explicitly, the action of a teacher consisting in the rational operation induced in the disciple which terminates in the knowledge of divine things. Now in so far as this action is a rational movement from principles to conclusions it is science in the process of its formation, science *in fieri*. Moreover, the movement from principle to conclusion and from conclusion to conclusion is at once the operation of science and the generation of the habit of science.

If it be true that St. Thomas does not change the subject of his consideration in the articles of the first question of the *Summa,* we may conclude *a priori* that sacred doctrine is science in the way that any doctrine which imparts a science can be called science. It is science in the process of its formation, *scientia in fieri;* for doctrine is the generation of science. Let us see whether this suggestion has any value.

In the *Sed contra*[1] of this article St. Thomas appeals to Augustine as his authority. Augustine says that to this science is attributed that by which faith is born, nourished, defended, and strengthened. This, says St. Thomas, pertains to no science other than sacred doctrine.

(1) *S. T.* I, 1, 2 : — *SED CONTRA EST* quod Augustinus dicit, XIV *de Trin.*: « Huic scientiae attribuitur illud tantummodo quo fides saluberrima gignitur, nutritur, defenditur, roboratur ». Hoc autem ad nullam scientiam pertinet nisi ad sacram doctrinam. Ergo sacra doctrina est scientia.

From this statement of St. Thomas we can see that he does not regard sacred doctrine either as the habit of sacred theology or the body of conclusions of theology. For to this science we must be able to attribute that by which faith is born. But neither the habit of sacred theology nor its conclusions can be said to give birth to faith, even though they can be said to nourish, defend, and strengthen it. However, the instruction in divine things by way of revelation not only nourishes, defends, and strengthens faith but also gives birth to faith, for faith results from the imperfect reception of this instruction.

Hence it would seem that St. Thomas is speaking of sacred doctrine as science in the process of its formation. For only in this sense can it be said to give birth to faith.

The body of this article [1] divides itself into two parts: 1) the statement that sacred doctrine is science; 2) the explanation of the sense in which it is science. In making precise this sense, St. Thomas says: « And in this way sacred doctrine is science, because it proceeds from principles known in the light of a superior science, namely the science of God and the blessed ».

The qualification which St. Thomas is explicitly making is that sacred doctrine is subalternated science, not non-subalternated science. However, apart from this qualification St. Thomas is also explicitly saying: « In this way sacred doctrine is science, because it proceeds from principles ».

It is difficult to determine with certainty whether he is here using the word science as the habit of science, or the generation or operation of science, or the conclusions of science. The illustrations from arithmetic, geometry, and music do not necessarily determine the sense, because the generation and operation of these habits as well as their conclusions proceed from principles; even the habits themselves can be said to proceed from principles. We may think when St. Thomas says that just as music believes the principles given it by arithmetic, so sacred doctrine believes the principles

(1) *S. T.* I, 1, 2c : — Respondeo. Dicendum sacram doctrinam esse scientiam. Sed sciendum est quod duplex est scientiarum genus. Quaedam enim sunt, quae procedunt ex principiis notis lumine naturali intellectus, sicut arithmetica, geometria, et huiusmodi. Quaedam vero sunt, quae procedunt ex principiis notis lumine superioris scientiae, sicut perspectiva procedit ex principiis notificatis per geometriam, et musica ex principiis per arithmeticam notis. Et hoc modo sacra doctrina est scientia, quia procedit ex principiis notis lumine superioris scientiae, quae scilicet est scientia Dei et beatorum. Unde sicut musica credit principia tradita sibi ab arithmetico, ita doctrina sacra credit principia revelata sibi a Deo.

revealed to it by God, that surely here he is speaking of the habit of knowledge. But properly speaking music itself does not believe anything; it is man who believes. And he believes in this case either in virtue of the habit (not that belief in this case is the function of the habit) or by reason of the generation of the habit in himself; for unless he believed the principles of arithmetic the habit of music could not be generated.

To those of us who have been reading this text for years in the light of the tradition set up by Cajetan and John of St. Thomas, it may seem to be forcing the text to allow the word science here to be interpreted as the generation of science, *scientia in fieri*. I thought so, too, for a long time. But now I can find nothing in St. Thomas which can certainly dislodge this interpretation.

In his other works St. Thomas frequently uses the word *scientia* in the sense of the generation or operation of science, the movement of reason from principle to conclusion and from conclusion to conclusion. We should note that the treatment of the nature of science itself in Aristotle occurs in the *Posterior Analytics* wherein is studied the third operation of intellect in regard to that which is proper to reason; that is to say, discourse, rational movement from one object of knowledge to another. Moreover, in St. Thomas' *Commentary on the Posterior Analytics* where he comments on the unity and diversity of science, he considers science from three points of view: 1) science, as rational movement from principles to conclusions (in this sense, doctrine is science); 2) science, as the effect of demonstration (in this sense, conclusions are science); 3) the habit of science [1].

(1) *In I Post. Anal.*, c. 28, lect. 41 (ed. Leon., I, pp. 305, 306).
— 7: Dicit ergo primo quod scientia dicitur una, ex hoc quod est unius generis subiecti. Cuius ratio est, quia processus scientiae cuiuslibet est quasi quidam motus rationis. Cuiuslibet autem motus unitas ex termino principaliter consideratur, ut patet in V *Physicorum*, et ideo oportet quod unitas scientiae consideretur ex fine sive ex termino scientiae. Est autem cuiuslibet scientiae finis sive terminus, genus circa quod est scientia : ...
8: ... Ad cuius evidentiam considerandum est quod, sicut iam dictum est, progressus scientiae consistit in quodam motu rationis discurrentis, ab uno in aliud: omnis autem motus a principio quodam procedit et ad aliquid terminatur; unde oportet quod in progressu scientiae ratio procedat ex aliquibus principiis primis. Si qua ergo res est, quae non habeat principia priora, ex quibus ratio procedere possit, horum non potest esse scientia, secundum quod scientia hic accipitur, prout est demonstrationis effectus. Unde scientiae speculativae non sunt de ipsis essentiis substantiarum separatarum. Non enim per scientias demonstrativas possumus scire *quod quid est* in eis ; ...
11: Ad huius ergo evidentiam sciendum est, quod materialis diversitas

93

Moreover, in the commentary *in Boethii de Trinitate*, question 6, where St. Thomas discusses the modes of speculative science, it is frequently impossible to understand the word *scientia* in any other sense than the generation of science, science in the process of its formation. Take for example the following text[1]:

Responsio. — Dicendum quod in scientiis speculativis semper ex aliquo prius noto proceditur, tam in demonstrationibus propositionum quam etiam in inventionibus definitionum. Sicut enim ex propositionibus praecognitis aliquis devenit in cognitionem conclusionis, ita ex conceptione generis et differentiae et causarum rei aliquis devenit in cognitionem speciei. Hic autem non est possibile in infinitum procedere, quia sic omnis scientia periret et quantum ad demonstrationes et quantum ad definitiones, cum infinita non sit pertransire. Unde omnis consideratio scientiarum speculativarum reducitur in aliqua prima, quae quidem homo non habet necesse addiscere aut invenire, ne oporteat in infinitum procedere, sed eorum notitiam naturaliter habet. Et huiusmodi sunt principia demonstrationum indemonstrabilia, ut 'omne totum est maius sua parte' et similia, in qua omnes demonstrationes scientiarum reducuntur, et etiam primae conceptiones intellectus, ut entis et unius et huiusmodi, in quae oportet reducere omnes definitiones scientiarum praedictarum.

Ex quo patet quod nihil potest sciri in scientiis speculativis neque per viam demonstrationis neque per viam definitionis nisi ea tantummodo, ad quae praedicta naturaliter cognita se extendunt. Huiusmodi autem naturaliter cognita homini manifestantur ex ipso lumine intellectus agentis, quod est homini naturale, quo quidem lumine nihil manifestatur nobis nisi in quantum per ipsum phantasmata fiunt intelligibilia in actu. Hic enim est actus intellectus agentis, ut dicitur in III *de Anima*[2] ...

Quidditas autem substantiarum separatarum non potest cognosci per ea quae a sensibus accipimus, ut ex praedictis patet, quamvis per sensibilia possumus devenire ad cognoscendum praedictas substantias esse et aliquas eorum conditiones. Et ideo per nullam scientiam speculativam potest sciri de aliqua substantia separata 'quid est', quamvis per scientias speculativas possimus scire ipsas esse et aliquas earum conditiones, ...

Thus in speaking of the procedure in science, of arriving at conclusions through science, St. Thomas is evidently using the term in the sense of the generation of science.

Hence I do not think it would be forcing St. Thomas' terminology in the slightest to understand the term *scientia* as predicated of sacred *doctrina* in the sense of the generation of science, the

obiecti non diversificat habitum, sed solum formalis. Cum ergo scibile sit proprium obiectum scientiae, non diversificabuntur scientiae secundum diversitatem materialem scibilium, sed secundum diversitatem eorum formalem ...

(1) *In Boethii de Trinitate*, q. 6, a. 4c, (ed. Wyser, pp. 74-75). Cf. also q. 6, a. 1c, pp. 55-57.

rational operation by which scientific knowledge is acquired. More-over, the understanding of the term *scientia* in this sense receives striking confirmation in the companion text to this article found in the *Commentary on the Sentences* [1].

> Ad aliud dicendum, quod, sicut habitus principiorum primorum non acqui-ritur per alias scientias, sed habetur a natura; sed acquiritur habitus conclusio-num a primis principiis deductarum; ita etiam in hac doctrina non acquiritur habitus fidei, qui est quasi habitus principiorum, sed acquiritur habitus eorum quae ex eis deducuntur et quae ad eorum defensionem valent...

Certainly in this text neither the word *scientia* nor the word *doctrina* can be understood in the sense of the habit of science. In both cases it refers to the operations by which the habit is acqui-red. For if in this doctrine a habit is acquired, then the doctrine is not the habit; the habit is rather the term of the doctrine.

Moreover, in the solution immediately preceding this response [2], it is clear that St. Thomas is considering sacred doctrine under

---

(1) *In I Sent.*, prol., q. 1, a. 3, sol. II, ad aliud [3m].
(2) *In I Sent.*, prol., q. 1, a. 3, sol. II: — ... vel dicendum quod in scientia duo est considerare, scilicet certitudinem, quia non quaelibet cognitio, sed cer-titudinalis tantum dicitur scientia; item quod ipsa est terminus disciplinae; omnia enim quae sunt in scientia ordinantur ad scire. Ex his autem duobus habet scientia duo. Ex primo habet quod est ex necessariis: ex contingentibus enim non potest causari certitudo; ex secundo quod est ex aliquibus principiis: sed hoc est di-versimode in diversis, quia superiores scientiae sunt ex principiis per se notis, sicut geometria, et huiusmodi habentia principia per se nota, ut: si ab aequa-libus aequalia deruas, etc. (a). Inferiores autem scientiae, quae superioribus su-balternantur, non sunt ex principiis per se notis, sed supponunt conclusiones probatas in superioribus scientiis, et eis utuntur pro principiis quae in veritate non sunt principia per se nota, sed in superioribus scientiis per principia per se nota probantur, sicut perspectiva quae est de linea visuali, et subalternatur geometriae a qua etiam supponit quae probantur de linea, inquantum linea, et per illa tanquam per principia probat conclusiones quae sunt de linea, inquantum visualis. Potest autem scientia aliqua esse superior alia dupliciter: vel ratione subiecti, ut geometria quae est de magnitudine, superior est ad perspectivam quae est de magnitudine visuali; vel ratione modi cognoscendi, et sic theologia est inferior scientia quae in Deo est. Nos enim imperfecte cognoscimus id quod ipse perfectissime cognoscit, et sicut scientia subalternata a superiori supponit aliqua, et per illa tamquam per principia procedit; sic theologia articulos fidei quae infallibiliter probati sunt in scientia Dei supponit, et eis credit, et per istud procedit ad probandum ulterius illa quae ex articulis sequuntur. Est ergo theo-logia scientia quasi subalternata divinae scientiae a qua accipit principia sua.
(We should note that this part of the solution which I have quoted is, very probably, an addition made by St. Thomas himself to his first redaction of the *Commentary*. Now although this fact may serve to indicate that the theory of subalternation was not perfectly worked out by St. Thomas at the time of the first redaction, it nevertheless throws light on St. Thomas' awareness of the dis-tinction between science as a habit and science as a discipline or doctrine. For indications that this text is an addition to the first redaction of the work, cf. M.-D. CHENU, *La théologie comme science*..., pp. 81-82).

the aspect of its procedure from principles and of its termination in certain conclusions of science. Here he begins his alternate solution by pointing out two characteristics of scientific knowledge: it is certain knowledge, and it is the term of discipline. Hence, he concludes that it must proceed from principles, from necessary principles. The rest of his discussion is concerned with the diversity of procedure in the formation or generation of subalternating and subalternated science. And he uses the term science sometimes to refer to its generation, sometimes to the knowledge or habit of knowledge involved.

However, in the answer to the third objection, St. Thomas states explicitly, as we have seem, that in this doctrine the habit of knowledge is acquired, thus indicating that the doctrine is not the habit, but the generation of the habit.

Thus although it is true that St. Thomas in the *Commentary* is not intent upon using either the term science or the term doctrine in their formal sense [1], he does indicate at least in one text the relation of the habit of sacred theology to the action he is administering [2]. In the *Summa*, however, where the fruit of his investigations about the function of a teacher and the action of divine instruction is sure to appear, we can expect to find that he is more conscious of the formal signification of the term *sacra doctrina*.

In concluding our discussion of this second article of the *Summa*, we may say that since there is no difficulty in understanding the term *scientia* here in the sense of science in the process of its formation, the subject term *sacra doctrina* may very well retain the sense we found it to have in the first article, i. e. instruction in divine things through revelation. Thus this instruction is science because it proceeds from the principles to the conclusions of science; this is true of any scientific doctrine.

On the other hand, to interpret the term science here in the sense of a habit of science, or a body of scientific conclusions, involves the difficulty of explaining how the habit of theological science or the body of conclusions deduced from the articles of

(1) Cf. for example, *In I Sent.*, prol., q. 1, a. 3, sol. I: where St. Thomas is speaking of sacred doctrine in its objective sense. Note, however, that he indicates he is considering this doctrine from the aspect of its term.

(2) In indicating this relationship St. Thomas himself confirms our interpretation of the meaning of *sacra doctrina* in the first article of the Commentary as *manuductio quaedam per cognitionem immediate ex divino lumine inspiratam in illam contemplationem quae perfecta erit in patria*. Cf. above p. 46.

faith can give birth to faith, an attribute that belongs to this science according to Augustine and St. Thomas. Secondly, if *sacra doctrina* is interpreted in the sense of a habit of knowledge, how then explain the *Commentary's* explicit statement that in this doctrine the habit of science is acquired. Thirdly, it is to be presumed that when St. Thomas begins to treat of one subject in a question he does not abandon that subject and treat of its analogate. And this presumption is not to be discarded without sufficient reason. Here there appears no reason for discarding the presumption. Fourthly, as the whole of the *Summa Theologica* is explicitly designed according to an order of discipline for the purpose of leading disciples through the steps of reasoning required to attain a scientific and sapiential knowledge of divine truth, we should be exceedingly careful not to discard that meaning of the term *sacra doctrina* which is eminently adapted to express the function of the *Summa*.

And finally, the great arguments brought against the scientific character of this divine science in the Middle Ages were that its principles were not self-evident, and that it did not proceed by reasoning from principles to conclusions [1]. The discussion about whether theology was science or not was concerned primarily with the formation or generation of the knowledge involved. And the term *scientia*, while it was employed to signify the habit of science, was also employed, and perhaps more commonly, to signify the process of reasoning by which conclusions are known with certainty. Hence we are not surprised to find Richard Kilwardby, for example, asking the following question about theology: « *Habito, quod sit scientia, quem habitum facit ?* »[2].

However, if in spite of these difficulties anyone should prefer to interpret the term *sacra doctrina* in the sense of some habit of science or some body of scientific conclusions, he should realize that this use of the term would be analogous to its use in the first article, not equivocal. For we have seen that the word *doctrina* which signifies formally the generation of science, can be used analogously by the analogy of attribution to signify its cause or its effect. Thus since sacred instruction generates as its effect a body of conclusions and hence a habit of science, the term *sacra*

(1) Cf. M.-D. Chenu, O.P., *La théologie comme science*..., pp. 33-53.
(2) *In Sent.*, prol., q. 13 (ed. Stegmüller, p. 44). Quoted from Chenu, *op. cit.*, p. 51.

7

doctrina may be used analogously to signify the effect produced by this instruction. We have already indicated the difficulties involved in this analogous interpretation of the term. The interpretation of the term as sacred instruction, the meaning we found it to have in the first article, does not involve these difficulties and hence should be considered at least more probable.

Now there still remains one point to be considered in this second article, which may be urged as an objection against our interpretation of the term *sacra doctrina.* In the second response Fr. Bonnefoy sees an identification of *sacra, doctrina* with *Sacra Scriptura.* If it is true that they are to be thus identified in this text, this would militate against interpreting the word *sacra doctrina* as an action, namely the instruction in divine things through revelation.

The response is as follows [1]:

Ad secundum. Dicendum quod singularia traduntur in sacra doctrina, non quia de eis principaliter tractatur; sed introducuntur tum in exemplum vitae, sicut in scientiis moralibus, tum etiam ad declarandum auctoritatem virorum per quos ad nos revelatio divina processit, super quam fundatur sacra scriptura seu doctrina.

It will also be worth while to quote Fr. Bonnefoy's comment on this text [2].

« Lui-même a pris soin, en répondant à l'objection, d'affirmer expressément leur équivalence dans la *Somme : sacra Scriptura seu doctrina.* Pouvait-il être plus explicite? L'équivalence implicitement contenue dans le *sed contra* de l'article 1er reçoit par la même une confirmation définitive. Et l'on voit du même coup, combien il serait arbitraire de détacher cet article du précédent.

L'on ne peut même pas expliquer la glose *seu doctrina* par une transcription due à l'inattention. Le passage parallèle du *Commentaire* ne contient rien de tel. Tout au contraire, saint Thomas a sacrifié, en abrégeant, l'expression *theologia* qui s'y trouvait trois fois.

L'équivalence entre *sacra Scriptura* et *sacra doctrina,* ici affirmée expressément, ressort tellement du contexte que les premiers copistes ont employé presque indifféremment une expression pour l'autre... ».

First, we must say that the fact that St. Thomas repeatedly adduces Sacred Scripture as evidence for what he says about *sacra*

(1) *S. T.,* I, 1, 2, ad 2.
(2) J. FR. BONNEFOY, O.F.M., *La nature de la théologie selon saint Thomas d'Aquin,* pp. 16-17.

doctrina does not necessarily imply that he is identifying the two. St. Thomas himself has indicated the relation between the written word and doctrine. .... *Scriptura enim ordinatur ad impressionem doctrinae in cordibus auditorum sicut ad finem* [1]. Now although the word *doctrina* itself in this context is used in the objective sense, *id quod docetur*, the expression *impressio doctrinae* signifies precisely that action which is the generation of knowledge, *doctrina* in its proper active sense. Therefore Scripture is ordered to the generation of divine knowledge.

Moreover, the written word in itself cannot be spoken of as doctrine except in so far as it is ordered to the impression of knowledge in another. For example, the words which a lad learning to type writes on the page as he practices his typing lesson is not doctrine. The written word is capable of receiving doctrine as its predicate only in so far as it is ordered to the generation of knowledge in another.

I will use an analogy to explain how it would be possible for St. Thomas to substitute the term *Sacra Scriptura* for *sacra doctrina* without identifying the two. The example I use is defective in many ways, but it is helpful to illustrate the one point I wish to clarify.

Suppose a mother is teaching her child to write. She may stand over him, take his hand in hers, and move it to form the letters in the proper way. Or she may take the pencil in her own hand and write the letters on a piece of paper for him to copy. And then if he doubts how a letter is to be formed, he can look at the paper. His playmate comes over to his house and sees him writing. « Oh, that's not the way to write that word », he says. « This is the way ».

« 'Tis not », says the other. « I 'll prove it to you ». And he shows him the piece of paper on which his mother had written the word. « This is the way to write it. ».

In brief, in order to prove he was writing the word the right way, he appeals to the example provided him by his mother. Certainly the example is not identical with the action of writing the word, but it is ordered to the writing of the word and shows how the word is to be formed. In his argument then it can be substituted for the correct writing of the word because of the authority which it carries.

(1) *S. T.*, III, 42, 4c.

This is a poor example in many respects. However, it does illustrate, I think, the point that when St. Thomas adduces the methods of Sacred Scripture as proof for the proper methods of sacred doctrine he is not necessarily identifying the Sacred Scripture with sacred doctrine, but appealing to an example *par excellence* which in itself is not sacred doctrine properly speaking but is ordered to sacred doctrine, shows how it proceeds, and serves as an infallible check on its procedure and methods.

Thus in the text of the response to the second objection in this article, we need not at all agree with Fr. Bonnefoy in seeing an identification of *sacra doctrina* with *Sacra Scriptura*. For the expression *Sacra Scriptura seu doctrina* in itself by no means necessarily signifies their identity in this text. Moreover, sacred doctrine understood as the generation of divine knowledge as well as Sacred Scripture which is ordered to the generation of this knowledge is founded on the revelation communicated by God to His prophets and apostles.

The Third Article

Having proved that sacred doctrine is science, because it proceeds from principles, St. Thomas pursues his investigation in the third article asking whether sacred doctrine is one science. The objections present the difficulties of uniting in the subject of one science Creator and creature and of finding a unity in a doctrine which treats of angels as well as corporal creatures and the actions of men.

After stating that sacred doctrine is one science, St. Thomas proceeds immediately to prove his statement. He appeals to the principle that the unity of a potency or habit must be judged from the unity of its formal object. For example, man, ass, and stone, though different things, agree in that which is the formal object of sight, — that which is colored. Now because Sacred Scripture considers some things under the aspect of their being divinely revealed, everything whatsoever that is divinely revealable shares in the one formal object of this science, and therefore is comprehended under sacred doctrine as under one science [1].

(1) *S. T.* I, 1, 3c : — Respondeo. Dicendum sacram doctrinam unam scientiam esse. Est unitas potentiae et habitus consideranda secundum obiectum, non quidem materialiter, sed secundum rationem formalem obiecti ; puta homo, asinus

At first sight, at least, St. Thomas here seems to be discussing sacred doctrine as if it were a habit of science. For although he does not say that sacred doctrine is a habit of science, he is certainly considering it in terms of the habit of science.

Let us see why. This artificial action, sacred instruction, supplies for the deficiency of the habit of theological science in the disciple, just as artificial respiration supplies for the deficiency of the power of respiration in a weak body [1]. Moreover, this instruction is not only guided and directed by the habit of sacred theology existing in the teacher, but is the operation of the habit as induced in the disciple. For the teacher induces in the disciple the same discourse of reason which he himself performs in his own intellect in virtue of his habit of science [2]. Thus sacred instruction arrives at the conclusions of the habit of sacred theology from the principles of the habit of sacred theology. Hence too, sacred instruction engages the objects of the habit of sacred theology under that aspect which is the formal object of the habit of sacred theology. For just as man, ass, stone etc., in so far as they are colored fall under the act of vision as under one potency, so Creator, creature, angel, man, etc., in so far as they are divinely revealable, fall under the operation, sacred instruction, as under the habit of one science.

Thus it seems quite proper that St. Thomas should judge the unity of sacred instruction from the principle of the unity of habit or potency. That he is proceeding in this way is indicated in the conclusion of his argument. He does not conclude that sacred doctrine is one habit of science, but that all things whatsoever that are divinely revealable are comprehended under sacred doctrine as under one habit of science: *sicut sub una scientia*.

Hence his reasoning may be understood as follows: Sacred instruction is one science (in operation), if all the things that it considers are comprehended under sacred instruction as they are under one habit of science. Now because sacred instruction considers all things whatsoever under the one formal aspect which constitutes the formal object of one habit of science, — namely,

et lapis conveniunt in una formali ratione colorati, quod est obiectum visus. Quia igitur Sacra Scriptura considerat aliqua secundum quod sunt divinitus revelata, secundum quod dictum est, omnia quaecumque sunt divinitus revelabilia, communicant in una ratione formali obiecti huius scientiae. Et ideo comprehenduntur sub sacra doctrina sicut sub una scientia.

(1) See above, pp. 67-68.
(2) See above, pp. 58-59.

their divine revealability, all things whatsoever are comprehended under this operation as under one habit of science. And hence sacred instruction is one science (in operation), just as vision is one potency (in operation).

The habit from which this operation proceeds exists only in the teacher. It will exist in the disciple as a result of the perfect reception of this operation from the teacher.

Hence sacred doctrine may very well maintain in the body of this third article the sense of instruction in divine things by way of revelation. It is one science (in operation) because all the objects which this operation engages fall under this operation as under one habit of science, just as vision is one potency (in operation) because all objects fall under vision as under one potency.

Now let us consider for a moment the answer to the second objection which can be urged as an objection against our interpretation of this article.

The second objection itself in concerned with showing that since sacred doctrine treats of things which pertain to the consideration of the philosophical sciences, it cannot be one science.

St. Thomas answers that nothing prevents the inferior potencies and habits from being diversified in regard to matters which fall under a single higher potency or habit, because the higher potency or habit regards the object under a more universal formality. Just as the object of the common sense is the sensible, which comprises under it the visible and the audible, so that the common sense, although one potency, extends to all objects of the five senses, likewise (in a similar manner) sacred doctrine existing as one can consider those things which are treated in the diverse philosophical sciences, in so far as they are divinely revealable, so that thus sacred doctrine is as it were a certain impression of the divine science, which is the one and simple science of all things [1].

---

(1) *S. T.* I, 1, 3, obj 2 & ad 2 : — Praeterea. In sacra doctrina tractatur de angelis, de creaturis corporalibus, de moribus hominum. Huiusmodi autem ad diversas scientias philosophicas pertinent. Igitur sacra doctrina non est una scientia.
. . . . .
Ad Secundum. Dicendum quod nihil prohibet inferiores potentias vel habitus diversificari circa illas materias, quae communiter cadunt sub una potentia vel habitu superiori ; quia superior potentia vel habitus respicit obiectum sub universaliori formali. Sicut obiectum sensus communis est sensibile, quod comprehendit sub se visibile et audibile ; unde sensus communis, cum sit una potentia, extendit se ad omnia obiecta quinque sensuum. Et similiter ea quae in

Here again St. Thomas may be judging the unity of sacred instruction as an operation of science from the principle of the unity of habit or potency. Just as nothing prevents the inferior potencies or habit from being diversified in regard to matter which falls under a single higher potency or habit, because the higher potency or habit regards the object under a more universal formality, LIKEWISE *(in a similar manner)* sacred instruction existing as one operation can engage the objects which fall under the operations of diverse philosophical sciences, in so far as these objects are divinely revealable, so that sacred instruction is a certain operation impressing, as it were, on the intellect the divine science which is the one and simple science of all things.

I realize that to understand the term *sacra doctrina* as sacred instruction and the term *impressio* in its active sense is contrary to all traditional interpretation. However, I do think that this interpretation is probable, especially if this article is considered in conjunction with the previous articles of the first question.

Moreover, there is some reason external to the context of the first question which may lead us to suspect that this active sense of the word *impressio* is the sense intended by St. Thomas. In the treatise on prophecy in the *Secunda Secundae* St. Thomas tells us that prophecy consists first and foremost in knowledge [1]. It is knowledge impressed on the intellect of the prophet from divine revelation by way of some sort of doctrine. The truth of this knowledge is the same in the disciple and in the teacher, because the knowledge of the disciple is an image of the knowledge of the teacher; just as in natural things the form generated is a certain likeness of the form which generated.

Respondeo. — Dicendum quod, sicut ex dictis patet, prophetia est *quaedam cognitio intellectui prophetae impressa ex revelatione divina per modum cuiusdam doctrinae.* Veritas autem cognitionis est eadem in discipulo et in docente, quia cognitio addiscentis est similitudo cognitionis docentis; sicut in rebus naturalibus forma generati est similitudo quaedam formae generantis ... [2].

diversis scientiis philosophicis tractantur, potest sacra doctrina una existens considerare sub una ratione, inquantum scilicet sunt divinitus revelabilia, ut sic sacra doctrina sit velut quaedam impressio divinae scientiae, quae est una et simplex omnium.

(1) *S. T.* II-II, 171, 1c.
(2) *S. T.,* II-II, 171, 6c (Italics here and in the following three citations are my own).

That there is question here of knowledge itself and not the generation of knowledge is clear. This knowledge comes from divine revelation and is comunicated by way of some sort of doctrine. Now in this article from which we have quoted, the expression *similitudo impressa* occurs three times to describe this knowledge and seems to be deliberately preferred to the term *impressio*, which also occurs, but is as well, even better understood in its active than in its passive sense, and is not used to describe this knowledge.

... Et ideo etiam prophetia, quae est *divinae praescientiae similitudo impressa* vel signum, qua immobili veritate futurorum contingentiam non excludit [1].

Ad Secundum. Dicendum quod divina praescientia respicit futura secundum duo : scilicet secundum quod sunt in seipsis, ... et secundum quod sunt in suis causis, ... Et quamvis ista duplex cognitio semper intellectui divino coniungatur, non tamen coniungitur in revelatione prophetica, quia *impressio agentis* non semper adaequat eius virtutem. Unde quandoque revelatio prophetica est *impressa quaedam similitudo divinae praescientiae* prout respicit futura contingentia in seipsis ... — Quandoque vero est *impressa similitudo divinae praescientiae,* prout scilicet cognoscit ordinem causarum ad effectus ... [2].

Moreover, a little farther on in the same treatise we find St. Thomas describing this likeness as the result of divine illumination, which is one means by which doctrine may be carried on.

... Sed huiusmodi illustratio mentis prophetica potest dici speculum inquantum resultat ibi *similitudo veritatis divinae praescientiae* [3].

As the *Secunda Secundae* was written several years after the *Pars Prima*, it would be unwise to regard this preference of *similitudo impressa* over *impressio divinae praescientiae* for signifying the knowledge of prophecy as any definite indication that the expression *impressio divinae scientiae* in the *Pars Prima* therefore carries an active sense. However, it does afford some reason why we should weigh carefully the probability of understanding the expression *impressio scientiae divinae* in its active meaning, especially since the context allows this interpretation.

It is true, however, that the text itself of this third article of the *Summa* readily lends itself to the interpretation of *sacra doctrina*

(1) *S. T.,* II, 171, 6, ad 1.
(2) *Ibid.* ad 2.
(3) *S. T.,* II-II, 173, 1c.

104

as habitual knowledge specified here as the habit of sacred theology. For we can substitute the term *habit of sacred theology* for *sacra doctrina* and get a good reading of the text. The term would thus be used analogously to its use as sacred instruction.

At this point we must regard both interpretations as probable. We should note well, however, that to accept the second interpretation by no means implies that St. Thomas uses the term equivocally in this question, as John of St. Thomas implies and as is explicitly stated by Fr. Chenu. The term would thus be used analogously to its use in the first question.

Articles four to six

There is no need for considering in detail the meaning of the term *sacra doctrina* in articles four, five, and six. For therein we meet the same problem of interpretation as in articles two and three. If *sacra doctrina* is understood formally as sacred instruction, i.e. the operation induced by the teacher in the disciple by way of revelation, then the term *scientia* is understood as the operation of science. If, however, the term *sacra doctrina* is understood analogously as a habit of knowledge, then the term *scientia* must signify the habit of science.

In article four, for example, *sacra doctrina* may be understood either as sacred instruction or as the habit of sacred theology. Understanding the term as signifying sacred instruction we read the text as follows :

Sacred instruction existing as one operation extends to those things which pertain to the diverse philosophical disciplines on account of the formal reason which it considers in diverse things, namely their cognoscibility by the divine light. Hence although among the philosophical sciences one is speculative while another is practical, nevertheless this operation of sacred instruction comprehends under it both, just as God by the same operation of science knows Himself and the things He makes.

However it is more speculative than practical, because it deals primarily with divine things rather than human acts. It deals with human acts in so far as through them man is ordered to the perfect knowledge of God in which eternal beatitude consists [1].

(1) *S. T.*, I, 1. 4c : — Respondeo. Dicendum quod sacra doctrina, ut dictum est, una existens se extendit ad ea quae pertinent ad diversas scientias philosophicas, propter rationem formalem quam in diversis attendit, scilicet prout sunt divino lumine cognoscibilia. Unde licet in scientiis philosophicis alia sit specu-

105

Now because of the analogy between habit and its operation, we can read this text substituting habit of science for operation of science without compromising the truth of what is said in any way.

The same is true of article five, where sacred doctrine is shown to excel all other sciences. However, here it becomes more clear that St. Thomas is talking about the operation of science induced by the teacher in the disciple and not about the habit of science. For he says that sacred doctrine employs the knowledge acquired through natural reason because our poor minds can more easily be led from this sort of knowledge to a knowledge of the things above reason imparted in this science [1]. Now a knowledge of divine things is not imparted in a habit of knowledge, but in an operation induced in a disciple. Hence it becomes clearer all along that St. Thomas is using the term *sacra doctrina* in its formal sense.

In the sixth article sacred doctrine is shown to be wisdom because in its most proper activity it determines truth about God in so far as He is the highest cause; moreover, it does this not only in regard to truth about God that is knowable through creatures, but also in regard to truth known to Himself alone and communicated to others through revelation [2]. Now all this can be

lativa et alia practica, sacra tamen doctrina comprehendit sub se utramque, sicut et Deus eadem scientia se cognoscit, et ea quae facit.

Magis tamen est speculativa quam practica, quia principalius agit de rebus divinis quam de actibus humanis, de quibus agit secundum quod per eos ordinatur homo ad perfectam Dei cognitionem, in qua aeterna beatitudo consistit.

(1) *S. T.*, I. 1, 5, ad 2: — Ad Secundum. Dicendum quod haec scientia accipere potest aliquid a philosophicis disciplinis, non quod ex necessitate eis indigeat, sed ad maiorem manifestationem eorum quae in hac scientia traduntur. Non enim accipit sua principia ab aliis scientiis, sed immediate a Deo per revelationem. Et ideo non accipit ab aliis scientiis tanquam a superioribus, sed utitur eis tanquam inferioribus et ancillis, sicut architectonicae utuntur subministrantibus, ut civilis militari. Et hoc ipsum quod sic utitur eis, non est propter defectum vel insufficientiam eius, sed propter defectum intellectus nostri; qui ex his quae per naturalem rationem ex qua procedunt aliae scientiae cognoscuntur, facilius manducitur in ea quae sunt supra rationem, quae in hac scientia traduntur.

(2) *S. T.*, I, 1, 6c: Respondeo. Dicendum quod haec doctrina maxime sapientia est inter omnes sapientias humanas, non quidem in aliquo genere tantum, sed simpliciter. Cum enim sapientis sit ordinare et iudicare, iudicium autem per altiorem causam de inferioribus habeatur; ille sapiens dicitur in unoquoque genere, qui considerat causam altissimam illius generis. Ut in genere aedificii artifex qui disponit formam domus, dicitur sapiens; et architector respectu inferiorum artificum, qui dolant ligna vel parant lapides; unde dicitur I *Cor.* III, 10: « Ut sapiens architector fundamentum posui ». Et rursus in genere totius humanae vitae prudens sapiens dicitur, inquantum ordinat humanos actus ad debitum finem; unde dicitur *Prov.*, X, 23: « Sapientia est viro prudentia ». Ille igitur qui consi-

said of the habit of sacred theology as well as of sacred instruction. For the habit of sacred theology is not merely a habit of science, but most properly a habit of wisdom, just as sacred instruction is not merely an operation of science, but most properly an operation of wisdom.

Articles seven and eight

In article seven St. Thomas discusses the subject of sacred doctrine. It is here that we find the key to the meaning of the term science as predicated of sacred doctrine in the first question of the *Summa*. St. Thomas begins by stating simply that God is the subject of this science. For the subject of science is related to science as object to habit or potency. Now the object of some potency or habit is properly assigned as the object under that aspect according to which all things are related to the habit or potency; for example, man and stone are related to the potency of sight in so far as they are colored; hence that which is colored is the proper object of sight. Now all things are treated in sacred doctrine under the aspect of God, either because they are God Himself, or because they are ordered to God as to their principle and end. Hence it follows that God is truly the subject of this science [1].

To find out what St. Thomas means by saying that the subject of science is related to science as object to potency or habit, let

derat simpliciter altissimam causam totius universi, quae Deus est, maxime sapiens dicitur: unde et sapientia dicitur divinorum cognitio, ut patet per Augustinum, XIII *de Trin.* Sacra autem doctrina propriissime determinat de Deo secundum quod est altissima causa; quia non solum quantum ad illud, quod est per creaturas cognoscibile, quod philosophi cognoverunt, ut dicitur *Rom.* I, 19: « Quod notum est Dei, manifestum est illis »; sed etiam quantum ad id quod notum est sibi soli de seipso, et aliis per revelationem communicatum. Unde sacra doctrina maxime dicitur sapientia.

(1) *S. T.*, I, 1, 7c: — Respondeo. Dicendum quod Deus est subiectum huius scientiae. Sic enim se habet subiectum ad scientiam, sicut obiectum ad potentiam vel habitum. Proprie autem illud assignatur obiectum alicuius potentiae vel habitus, sub cuius ratione omnia referuntur ad potentiam vel habitum, sicut homo et lapis referuntur ad visum inquantum sunt colorata, unde coloratum est proprium obiectum visus. Omnia autem pertractantur in sacra doctrina sub ratione Dei, vel quia sunt ipse Deus, vel quia habent ordinem ad Deum, ut ad principium et ad finem. Unde sequitur quod Deus vere sit subiectum huius scientiae. — Quod etiam manifestum fit ex principiis huius scientiae, quae sunt articuli fidei, quae est de Deo; idem autem est subiectum principiorum et totius scientiae, cum tota scientia virtute contineatur in principiis.

us turn to his *Commentary on the Posterior Analytics* [1]. Here St. Thomas discusses the unity and diversity of science from two points of view; 1) science as an operation, a movement from principle to term; 2) science as a habit. The unity of science as a movement of reason from principles to conclusions is to be judged from the unity of the formal subject in which the movement terminates; for the term of any science is the knowledge of its subject. The unity of a habit of science, however, is to be judged from the unity of its formal object.

These two points of view from which a science can be regarded have given rise to much confusion concerning the terms formal subject and formal object of science. There was no confusion in St. Thomas' mind on this point.

The subject of a science is the term of the movement of science. For the process of any science is, as it were, a certain movement of reason passing from one thing to another. As every movement proceeds from some principle and ends at some term, so in the operation of science reason proceeds from some principle and ends at some term. The unity of any movement is to be judged principally from the unity of its term; for example, the reason why this line (—) is one is that it has one term. Likewise the reason why the operation of any science is one is that it has one term. But the term of any operation of science is the subject which the science is about. Hence the unity of the operation of any science is to be judged from the unity of its subject [2].

The diversity of the operations of science, however, is not to be judged from their subjects alone, but primarily from their principles. For, as was said above, the progress of science consists in a certain movement of reason advancing from one thing to another. Now although the unity of movement is to be judged primarily from its term, the reason for the diversity of movements in found primarily in their principles. The reason why these two lines, for

(1) *In I Post. Anal.*, cc. 27-29, lect. 41 (ed. Leon., I, pp. 303-307).
(2) *In I Post. Anal.*, c. 28, lect. 41 (ed. Leon., I, p. 305): — 7. Dicit ergo primo quod scientia dicitur una, ex hoc quod est unius generis subiecti. Cuius ratio est, quia processus scientiae cuiuslibet est quasi quidam motus rationis. Cuiuslibet autem motus unitas ex termino principaliter consideratur, ut patet in V *Physicorum*, et ideo oportet quod unitas scientiae consideretur ex fine sive ex termino scientiae. Est autem cuiuslibet scientiae finis sive terminus, genus circa quod est scientia: ...Unde relinquitur quod cuiuslibet scientiae unitas secundum unitatem subiecti est attendenda. ...

example, (>) are not one is not found in their term considered by itself, because the point in which they terminate is materially common to both. The reason is found rather in the terms as they are related to their principles. Hence we find the distinction of these lines primarily in their principles: also, however, in their terms if formally considered, i.e. as related to their principles.

Likewise the diversity of the operations of science is not to be judged from their subjects considered merely in themselves. These may be materially the same. It is to be judged rather from their subjects considered in relation to their principles. Hence the diversity of the operations of science is to be judged primarily from their principles; also however, from their subjects if formally considered, i.e. in relation to their principles [1].

Hence if a science (operation) has one kind of principles, it will have one kind of subject. If it has one kind of subject, it must have one kind of principles. For the unity of the subject and of its principles correspond to each other.

We are now able to state clearly the terms of the proportion set up by St. Thomas in the article of the *Summa* under discussion. The proportion is represented thus:

$$\frac{\text{science}}{\text{subject}} \quad :: \quad \frac{\text{potency}}{\text{object}} \quad :: \quad \frac{\text{habit}}{\text{object}}$$

It is to be read as follows: The subject of the operation of science stands in relation to the operation of science as object to

---

(1) *In I Post. Anal.*, c. 28, lect. 41 (ed. Leon., I, pp. 305-307):
— 8. ... Ad cuius evidentiam considerandum est quod, sicut iam dictum est, progressus scientiae consistit in quodam motu rationis discurrentis ab uno in aliud: omnis autem motus a principio quodam procedit et ad aliquid terminatur; unde oportet quod in progressu scientiae ratio procedat ex aliquibus principiis primis. ...
10. ... cum rationem unitatis scientiae acceperit ex unitate generis subiecti, rationem diversitatis scientiarum non accepit ex diversitate subiecti, sed ex diversitate principiorum. Dicit enim quod una scientia est altera ab alia, quarum principia sunt diversa; ita quod nec ambarum scientiarum principia procedant ex aliquibus principiis prioribus, nec principia unius scientiae procedant ex principiis alterius; quia sive procederent ex eisdem principiis, sive alia ex aliis, non esset diversa scientia.
13. ... Ad hoc autem quod principia indemonstrabilia sunt unius generis, accipitur ut signum [unitatis generis scibilis], cum ea quae demonstrantur per ipsa, sint in eodem genere et congenea, idest connaturalia vel proxima secundum genus sibi ipsis; huiusmodi enim habent eadem principia. Et sic patet quod unitas generis scibilis, in quantum est scibile, ex quo accipiebatur unitas scientiae, et unitas principiorum, secundum quam accipiebatur scientiae diversitas, sibi mutuo correspondent.

potency and as object to habit. Since St. Thomas is speaking of the formal object in relation to potency and habit, as is clear from his example of the potency of sight, the corresponding term in his proportion must be the formal subject of science. For by no stretch of the imagination could he be interpreted as saying that the material subject of the operation of science stands in relation to the operation of science as formal object to potency or habit.

This proportion is valid, because just as the formal object is the principle of unity of potency or habit, so the formal subject is the principle of unity in the operation of science. Actually the formal subject in which the movement of science terminates is objectively identical with the formal object of the habit of science concerned. As principle of unity for the operation this « scibile » is called subject; as principle of unity for habit it is called object.

St. Thomas specifies the formal subject of sacred doctrine as God. He gives little explanation except that all other things besides God are considered in this science only in so far as they are related to God as to their principle and end. He has said the same thing before in article three [1]. Moreover, in the third article St. Thomas has also specified for us the formal aspect of the subject of this operation of science which is objectively the formal aspect of the object of the habit of this science. For this he invented the term *revelabile*. We may wonder why St. Thomas does not mention revelability again in article seven when speaking of the formal subject of sacred doctrine. Actually he does not need to mention it again. Moreover, to specify the formal subject of sacred doctrine as God is in itself sufficient, because this operation of science is the only one accessible to man in his present state (according to God's ordinary providence) which has God for its subject. For the doctrine of natural theology, the only science with which sacred doctrine could be confused, does not have God for its subject. God is the first and final cause of its subject; hence God is considered in natural theology *non tamquam subiectum scientiae sed tamquam*

(1) *S. T.*, I, 1, 3, ad 1: — Ad Primum Ergo. Dicendum quod sacra doctrina non determinat de Deo et de creaturis ex aequo, sed de Deo principaliter, et de creaturis secundum quod referuntur ad Deum, ut ad principium vel finem. Unde unitas scientiae non impeditur. — (That he is here speaking of the subject of sacred doctrine is clear from the objection).

principium subiecti [1]. Hence in saying that God is the subject of sacred doctrine, St. Thomas has said enough [2].

To obtain an adequate understanding of the formal object of the habit of sacred theology according to St. Thomas, article seven of the first question of the *Summa* must be considered in its proper relation with article three. We cannot go into the question of the formal object of this habit here, since to do more than to determine the reality which is named by *sacra doctrina* is beyond the scope we have set for ourselves in this present study. However, I would like to remark that the man who, is my opinion, has approached most closely to the true notion of the object of sacred theology according to St. Thomas is M. Gilson, even though he has not attempted any definition of sacred theology [3]. It should be noted, however, that what he says about the term *revelabile* is open to misunderstanding on the part of the reader. For one may be misled to think that according to M. Gilson natural knowledges *only*, and as included in the body of revelation are to be included under the term *revelabilia*, that all knowledge in itself beyond the powers of human reason is to be spoken of as *revelatum* [4]. This is *not* what he means, I am sure. But if one does not bear in mind the nature of the work M. Gilson is doing, he may unfortunately take this meaning from his words.

(1) Cf. *In Boethii de Trin.*, q. 5, a. 4c, (ed. Wyser, p. 48): — « Sic ergo theologia sive scientia divina est duplex; una, in qua considerantur res divinae non tamquam subiectum scientiae, sed tanquam principia subiecti, et talis est theologia, quam philosophi prosequuntur, quae alio nomine metaphysica dicitur; alia vero, quae ipsas res divinas considerat propter seipsas ut subiectum scientiae, et haec est theologia, quae in sacra Scriptura traditur ... ». We should note two things about this text: first, it represents a development in Thomas' thought since he wrote the *Commentary on the Sentences* (cf. *In I Sent.*, prol., q. 1, a. 3, Sol. I), where he indicated that God is also the subject of metaphysics; second, the correct reading of the text according to the autograph Cod. Vat. lat. 9850, as edited by Paul Wyser, O.P., is ... *theologia, quae in sacra Scriptura traditur* ..., not *theologia, quae sacra Scriptura dicitur*, the reading which Fr. Bonnefoy uses in trying to demonstrate his definition of *sacra doctrina* (*op. cit.*, p. 14). ·

(2) Cf. E. GILSON, *L'être et l'essence*, Paris: J. Vrin, 1948, pp. 78-88. His discussion, I think, would have been helped along considerably by the use of the text of St. Thomas cited in note 1.

(3) E. GILSON, *Le Thomisme*⁵. Paris: J. Vrin, 1947, cf. Introduction, pp. 8-41.

(4) E. GILSON, *Le Thomisme*⁵. Paris: J. Vrin, 1947, cf. Introduction, p. 23: « ... ces connaissances naturelles, incluses dans le corps de la révélation, appartiennent à l'ordre de ce que saint Thomas d'Aquin nomme le *revelabile*. Ce « révélable » est donc du philosophique entraîné, pour ainsi dire, dans l'orbite de la théologie, parce que comme celle du révélé, la connaissance en est nécessaire au salut. A la différence du « révélé », le « révélable » ne figure pas dans la théologie de plein droit et en vertu de sa propre essence, mais comme inclus dans la révélation; qui l'assume en vue de sa propre fin ».

For our purpose, the most important conclusion to be drawn from our discussion of this seventh article of the first question of the *Summa* is that this article provides us with the key to the proper interpretation of article three. The interpretation which we have suggested for article three now becomes manifestly the correct interpretation. We said that in the third article St. Thomas was considering the unity of sacred doctrine in terms of the habit of science, because the unity of the operation of science is similar to the unity of the habit of science. For St. Thomas' conclusion in that article is not that sacred doctrine is one habit of science, but that its unity is similar or analogous to the unity of one habit of science: ... *omnia quaecumque sunt divinitus revelabilia ... comprehenduntur sub sacra doctrina sicut sub una scientia.* The reason for the validity of this analogy is found in the proportion stated in article seven. For just as the formal subject of the operation of science is the principle of unity for the operation, so the formal object of habit or potency is the principle of unity for habit or potency.

Thus although the third article considered in itself is capable of two interpretations, nevertheless considered in the context of the other articles of the first question, it can bear only that interpretation which we have given. Hence too, it becomes perfectly clear that the reality which St. Thomas names by the term *sacra doctrina* and which forms the subject of this first question is the ACTION, sacred instruction in divine things. This action is necessary for man's salvation (art. 1). It is an operation of science (art. 2), one operation (art. 3), both speculative and practical (art. 4), the most noble of all operations of science (art. 5), an operation of wisdom (art. 6). The subject of this operation is God (art. 7).

In the eighth article St. Thomas shows that this operation is argumentative. There is no need to investigate this article in detail because it is perfectly obvious that he is here speaking of the operation in which divine knowledge is acquired and hence of *sacra doctrina* in its formal sense.

Articles nine and ten.

The presence of two articles about Sacred Scripture in the first question of the *Summa* has been the source of much difficulty especially among those who would like to regard this question primarily as a treatise on the nature of the habit of theological science. Fr. Chenu, for example, goes so far as to say that the introduction of these questions was merely a concession made by St. Thomas to the usage of the time, and that the internal logic of his theory would in the course of time eliminate them [1].

If, however, we understand this first question as a treatise about instruction in divine things by way of revelation, we can understand how these two questions belong to this treatise.

Sacred Scripture is immediately ordered to the impression of God's own knowledge on our intellects. It is one of the means by which God carries on the instruction of men in the things of salvation. God provides for His creatures according as it befits their nature. Now as it is natural for men to come to the knowledge of spiritual reality by way of sensible reality, it is fitting that God should clothe in figures from sensible reality the spiritual truths that He teaches us. Moreover, this procedure is especially in place in Sacred Scripture, since it is directed to all men, regardless of their level of intellectual development. This « picture method » if I may call it such, is a universal method, pleasant as well as suitable for all men. St. Thomas explains all this for us in the ninth article.

However, men of different degrees of intelligence illumined by different degrees of supernatural light understand in different degrees the truths that are proposed in Sacred Scripture. It is true that since it is the word of God, all should be prepared to accept what is said purely and simply on the authority of God. We do well sometimes to learn what is said and simply believe it. In many, however, this instruction terminates in nothing more than faith. Yet God's own desire is that this knowledge pass beyond faith to a certain understanding and contemplation of the truths He teaches about Himself. Hence we find Scripture frequently proceeding by way of argumentation, giving reasons in virtue of which the truths presented can be understood. And in presenting these arguments God does not want us merely to believe that this truth can be proved. He wants us to *see* and to *understand* in so far as we are able.

Now although it is proper for all instruction in divine things to employ analogous concepts owing to the nature of man, it is peculiarly proper that Sacred Scripture employ figures from sensible

(1) See above, p. 33.

113

8

reality, because it is ordered to the instruction of all men regardless of the degree of their intellectual development. The instruction of those who are more intelligent, such as for example is carried on through the instrumentality of teachers of sacred theology, though it necessarily begins with images from sensible things, rises in so far as possible above these sensible images in striving for a more perfect understanding of divine truth. Hence this instruction is carried on in terms of reality that is more intelligible than sensible reality. Moreover, the order followed in this advanced instruction will be different from the order of Scripture.

Scripture itself in great part is narrative. The method of narration used in giving instruction is always closely associated with the picture method. Both can be termed universal methods, and hence very well suited to the purpose of Sacred Scripture. The method of the *Summa Theologica,* however, is the method of discipline, the order of principles to conclusions, an order which is adapted not to all men but only to those capable of pursuing a science.

Yet, even in the instruction of the more intelligent the Scriptures always serve not only as an infallible guide, but in conjunction with Tradition they are the perennial source of supernatural truth for men, just as the natural objects of sense are the perennial source of all natural knowledge. And just as the pursuit of natural knowledge ends in sterility and tragedy when it loses contact with the natural objects of sense, so with the pursuit of supernatural knowledge when contact is lost with the Scriptures. Scripture then must always be maintained as the basic text of sacred instruction even when this instruction is carried on through the instrumentality of the teachers of theology.

Hence it is not difficult to see the relation between Sacred Scripture and sacred doctrine. They are not identical, but one is ordered to the other, just as the negative of a photograph is ordered to the printing of the positive.

In the ninth article, however, St. Thomas speaks of Sacred Scripture and sacred doctrine in a way that might suggest that he considers them identical. For example, he speaks of sacred doctrine making use of metaphor as well as of Sacred Scripture making use of metaphor. Moreover, in the *Sed Contra* he argues that since Sacred Scripture uses methaphor, it belongs to sacred doctrine to use it.

Sed contra est quod dicitur *Osee* XII, 10: « Ego visionem multiplicavi eis, et manibus prophetarum assimilatus sum ». Tradere autem aliquid sub similitudine est metaphoricum. Ergo ad sacram doctrinam pertinet uti metaphoris.

. . . . .

. . . Sed sacra doctrina utitur metaphoris propter necessitatem et utilitatem, ut dictum est. (ad 1).

True, it is possible to interpret the term *sacra doctrina* in these instances as Sacred Scripture. For Sacred Scripture in so far as it is ordered to the instruction of men in the things of God can be called *sacra doctrina* by analogy. Does St. Thomas intend this analogous use of the term? I think not. The term can very well maintain its formal sense. For the rational operation which the teacher induces in his disciple can be said to make use of metaphor as well as the verbal discourse of the teacher. Moreover, from the use of metaphor in Sacred Scripture one can conclude to the propriety of its use in the rational discourse which the human teacher of divine knowledge induces instrumentally in his disciple.

Then, too, in article ten, which is devoted exclusively to the manifold sense of the text of Sacred Scripture, the term *sacra doctrina* does not occur. This is very significant, I think, because article ten is the only article of the first question in which the term *sacra doctrina* or its equivalent *haec doctrina* does not appear. If St. Thomas had been using *sacra doctrina* in the ninth and preceding articles for *Sacra Scriptura*, why does he suddenly stop using it in the tenth article? The explanation is clear if we allow sacred doctrine to retain its formal sense in the preceding articles.

Since the author of Sacred Scripture is God Himself, who has the power to adapt and use not only words to signify His thought, but even things themselves, Scripture can carry a manifold spiritual sense as well as a literal sense. These various senses of Scriptures must be explained by the teachers of the Church who carry on this instruction by ministering His inspired Word to men. Hence, the discussion of the manifold sense of the Scriptures is very much in place in this or any other treatise about sacred doctrine. St. Thomas reserves the tenth article of the first question for this discussion.

Scripture, then, is the book written by God Himself for instructing His children in the knowledge of salvation. It is the sacred writing of this instruction: *Sacra Scriptura huius doctrinae* [1]. It is

(1) *S. T.*, I. 1, introd.

the first and most fundamental book upon which all other books of sacred instruction depend.

In so far as sacred instruction involves the exposition of the sense of God's word, this action which St. Thomas has already described as an operation of science, etc., is also an operation of exegesis, or we may say, an operation of the art of literary criticism. This point, too, could be proved from the Scriptures, as there we find Our Lord, for example, explaining the sense of His parables to His Apostles and unfolding the Scriptures to the two disciples on the way to Emmaus.

The question which is bound to bother the reader is how this one operation of sacred instruction can be an operation of science, both speculative and practical, an operation of wisdom, and also an operation of exegesis. Here I can only say that the unity in question here is a unity of operation, not a unity of essence [1]. The adequate answer has been given to us by St. Thomas. But if we are to judge from the writings of theologians since his time, I think we must admit that the ages which have intervened between St. Thomas and the present did not know this answer. The lack of unity which theologians thought they saw in the first question of the *Summa Theologica* is symbolic of the lack of unity in theology itself since the thirteenth century. The seamless garment of Christian wisdom has been rent asunder since the Middle Ages and with it the unity of our Christian civilization. It was Thomas who first discovered in a definable way the unifying principle of all activity both speculative and practical in the order of salvation. During the centuries which followed this discovery was not appreciated. Men of learning, theologians included, took to the pursuit of history and science for the solutions of their problems. And thus they have answered a good many questions. But the order of knowledges and hence the order of living was not clearly perceived. This order in which peace and salvation is found is the order of divine wisdom which comes to man through sacred instruction under which all things whatsoever fall as under the habit of Christian wisdom. Moreover, this order will never be rediscovered adequately so long as theology is regarded

(1) As an introductory study to this question I suggest G. P. Klubertanz S.J., « The Unity of Human Activity », *The Modern Schoolman*, XXVII (1950), pp. 75-103.

merely in terms of theological conclusions or in terms of history or in terms of literary criticism. It will be rediscovered when theology is once again regarded as it was by St. Thomas as the habit of Christian wisdom.

To say even this much about the unity of this operation called sacred doctrine is going beyond the scope of our work. However, I considered it necessary to indicate in general the kind of unity which is found in the operation called sacred doctrine.

CHAPTER IV

CONCLUSION AND SUMMARY

Our purpose in this study was to determine the subject of the first question of the *Summa Theologica*, the reality named by St. Thomas by the term *sacra doctrina*. We have discovered that this reality is an action, the instruction of men in the knowledge of salvation. We have seen that St. Thomas has described this action as necessary for salvation, an operation of science, one operation which is both speculative and practical, an operation of wisdom. The subject of this operation is God. Yet it extends to all other things, even those considered in the philosophical disciplines, in so far as they are related to God as their principle and end. In so far as sacred doctrine involves the exposition of the sense of God's word it is also an operation of the art of literary criticism.

Thus sacred doctrine is at once the generation of the habit of sacred theology, the acquired habit of supernatural wisdom. To the generation of this Christian wisdom God has ordained the Scriptures, just as natural existing things are ordered to the generation of natural wisdom.

Hence sacred doctrine is not to be identified with Sacred Scripture, nor is it to be identified with the habit of sacred theology. It is doctrine in the formal sense of the term: i.e. the generation of knowledge, an operation induced in the intellect of the disciple terminating in new knowledge acquired. The human teacher administers sacred doctrine as an instrumental cause. The principal cause of this operation is God who through a complexity of instrumental causes leads man to a knowledge of Himself in this life which is proportioned to the knowledge in which his final beatitude consists.

This operation of God in the intellects of his human children,

118

administered by the *magisterium* of His Church, proceeding under the light of faith, terminating in divine and supernatural wisdom as it is possible for men on earth, — this operation is the instruction of men in the knowledge of salvation. This is the reality which is the subject of discussion in the first question of the *Summa Theologica* and which is signified by St. Thomas under the term *sacra doctrina*.

For this is clearly the meaning of the term in the first article of the question. It is the meaning in which the term must be understood throughout the first question, unless St. Thomas is to be accused of beginning to discuss one subject and then straightway abandoning it without any warning to discuss another subject. This meaning gives unity and coherence to the whole question and in no way forces or does violence to the text. Moreover, to understand the term in this meaning clears up difficulties that have been bothering theologians for centuries; — especially the relation between Sacred Scripture and sacred doctrine and the habit of theology.

We might crystallize the work we have done in the following demonstration :

In any question written by an author of the calibre of St. Thomas, that meaning must be accepted for the term used to signify the subject of his investigation which is clearly indicated in the beginning, which gives unity and coherence to the whole discussion without doing any violence to the text, and which is demanded for the full appreciation of what the author is saying.

But in the case in question, the meaning which is clearly indicated in the beginning, which gives unity and coherence to the whole investigation without doing violence to the text, and which is demanded for the full appreciation of what the author is saying is the action of instructing men in the knowledge of salvation. Hence the meaning which must be accepted for the term *sacra doctrina* in the first question of the *Summa Theologica* is the action of instructing men in the knowledge of salvation.

The major of this demonstration is self-evident.

The minor has been adequately proved in the body of this study.

The conclusion I regard as certain.

I have avoided in so far as I was able the discussion of the relation of sacred doctrine to revelation. What I did say about it was sufficient for my purpose. However, if one examines the nature of revelation according to St. Thomas as a divine action, instead of considering it in terms of the written or spoken word instrumental in this divine action, he shall see that according to St. Thomas sacred doctrine is a participated form of divine revelation. In its perfection it is the unmediated divine action in the blessed in heaven. In a lower and more complex form it is the mediated divine action in the prophets. In a still lower and still more complex form it is the instruction of men in the knowledge of salvation. Thus sacred doctrine is revelation. For revelation in this sense signifies the same reality as sacred doctrine but according to its proper mode.

However, this must be properly understood. Sacred doctrine as a participation of prophetic revelation will never bring to man any truth that was not communicated to the prophets and apostles. The deposit of revealed truth was closed with the death of the last Apostle. But the unfolding of this truth to men through sacred doctrine will continue till the last day. This teaching of St. Thomas is thoroughly in accord with the teachings of the Church. If not, I would reject it immediately as St. Thomas would have done, had he thought it in conflict with our faith.

It is my hope that this study will lead to a fuller appreciation of the unity of the *Summa Theologica* of St. Thomas, and hence to the rediscovery of the unity of theology itself, which has suffered unbelievably from its being divided up into various parts.

I am confident that with the true appreciation of sacred theology as Christian wisdom, theology will be restored to its position of eminence in *all* our Catholic Universities. The term *Catholic education* which is only the modern translation of the term *sacred doctrine* will then come to signify in our modern world the fullness of the reality it is intended to cover. Theology will no longer be regarded as something properly for clerical students and yet condescendingly offered to the laity under such baiting titles as « Theology for the Layman ». That title reminds me of the advertisement, « Long Pants for Boys ». The assumption in this advertisement, of course, is that boys have no right to wear long pants, but here is an opportunity for them at least to look grown up. The Christian wisdom of sacred theology is not only something to which all men have a right. They have the duty to pursue it since in this wisdom is found the order of *all things whatsoever* to their

120

final end, and through this wisdom is achieved that peace and tranquillity of order which is above all understanding.

All of us whose vocation it is to be teachers of sacred theology will do well to take the same care in our teaching as did St. Thomas. In beginning his work he first considered what sort of action he was to administer, the qualities of this operation, its formal subject, and to what things it extended. He also had clearly in mind the capacity of the subjects in whom this action was to be received. He then proceeded to order his work in a manner adapted to their capacity, in this case following the order of discipline. Here it is not a question merely of removing doubts from the minds of his disciples, but of leading them to the understanding of truth.

Quaedam vero disputatio est magistralis in scholis non ad removendum errorem, sed ad instruendum auditores ut inducantur ad intellectum veritatis quam intendit : et tunc oportet rationibus inniti investigantibus veritatis radicem, et facientibus scire *quomodo sit verum* quod dicitur : alioquin si nudis auctoritatibus magister quaestionem determinet, certificabitur quidem auditor quod ita est, sed nihil scientiae vel intellectus acquiret et vacuus abscedet [1].

Hence it should be clear why St. Thomas deliberately preferred to use the term *sacra doctrina* instead of *theologia* in the first question of his *Summa*. For he is thereby naming the action which he is to administer through the words that he writes. He is using the term with a fulness of appreciation undreamt of by his predecessors (and we might add his successors) in the Middle Ages. It may be true that he did not fully appreciate the meaning of the term when he wrote the *Commentary*, as the tendency there was to limit the meaning of the word to the communication of divine truth in its scientific and sapiential aspects. However, by the end of his first teaching period at Paris, after he had written the *De Veritate* and his commentary *In Boethii de Trinitate*, his appreciation of the term *sacra doctrina* and the nature of the action it signifies was almost, if not entirely, complete.

(1) *Quaest. Quodl.,* qd. 4, q. 9, art. 3 (18).

BIBLIOGRAPHY (¹)

ADAMCZYK, STANISLAUS, *De obiecto Formali Intellectus Nostri secundum doctrinam S. Thomae Aquinatis. (Analecta Gregoriana*, Vol. II). Romae: apud Aedes Pontificiae Universitatis Gregorianae, 1933, pp. xv-152.

BILLUART, C. R., O.P., *Summa Sancti Thomae Hodiernis Academiarum Moribus Accommodata....* Editio nova. Parisiis-Lugduni: Lecoffre, 1878, 10 vol.

BILZ, J., *Einführung in die Theologie. Theologische Enzyklopädie*, Freiburg: Herder, 1935, pp. VII-167.

BONNEFOY, J.-Fr., O.F.M., *La Nature de la Théologie selon saint Thomas d'Aquin.* Paris: J. Vrin, 1939, pp. 88. Previously printed as: « La théologie comme science et l'explication de la foi selon S. Thomas d'Aquin », *Ephemerides Theologicae Lovanienses*, XIV (1937), pp. 421-446; 600-631; XV (1938), pp. 491-516.

— « La méthodologie théologique de saint Thomas », *Revista Española de Teologia*, X (1950), pp. 41-81.

BOURKE, VERNON J., *Thomistic Bibliography*. St. Louis: (*The Modern Schoolman* Suppl. to Vol. XX), 1945, pp. VIII-312.

BOYER, CHARLES, S. J., « Qu'est-ce que la théologie », *Gregorianum*, XXI (1940), pp. 255-266.

CAJETANUS, THOMAS DE VIO CARD., O.P., *Commentarii in Summam Theologiae S. Thomae Aquinatis*, in S. Thomae Aq. *Opera Omnia jussu impensaque Leonis XIII, P.M., edita.* Romae: R. Garroni, 1882-Vols. IV-XII.

CATHALA, M. P., (ed.), *S. Thomae in Metaphysicam Aristotelis Commentaria.* Turin: Marietti, 1935, pp. xii-798.

CERVO, P., « La teologia como ciencia », *Ciencia Tomista*, XLVI (1932), pp. 173-199.

CHARLIER, L., O.P., *Essai sur le problème théologique.* Thuillies: Ramgall, 1938, p. 189. (Cf. decree of Holy Office, Feb. 4, 1947, *AAS* (1942) p. 37).

CHENU, M.-D., O.P., *Une école de théologie.* Etoiles: Le Saulchoir, 1937. (Cf. decree of Holy Office, Feb. 4, 1942, *AAS* (1942), p. 37.

— « Un essai de méthode théologique au XII siècle », *Revue des Sciences Philosophiques et Théologiques*, XXIV (1935), pp. 258-267.

---

(1). In this bibliography I am including some works discussing the nature of theology and the present position of theology which are helpful for a better understanding of the problem of the unity of theology.

CHENU, M.-D., O.-P., « Grammaire et théologie aux XIIe et XIIIe siècles », *Archives d'Histoire Doctrinale et Littéraire du Moyen-Age.*

— *Introduction à l'étude de S. Thomas d'Aquin.* Montréal : Institut d'Études Médiévales; Paris : J. Vrin, 1950, pp. 305.

— « Le plan de la Somme théologique de S. Thomas », *Revue Thomiste,* XLV (1939), pp. 93-107.

— « Position de la théologie », *Revue des Sciences Philosophiques et Théologiques,* XXIV (1935), pp. 232-257.

— « La psychologie de foi, dans la théologie du XIIIe siècle », *Publications de l'Institut d'Études Médiévales d'Ottawa,* Vol. II, pp. 163-192.

— « La théologie comme science au XIIIe siècle », *Archives d'Histoire Doctrinale et Litteraire du Moyen-Age,* II (1927), pp. 31-71. Enlarged, revised, and re-edited as *La théologie comme science au XIIIe siècle.* Pro manuscripto. Paris : J. Vrin, 1943, pp. 123.

CONGAR, M.-J., [Comptes rendus], *Bulletin Thomiste,* XV (1938-1939) pp. 490-505, 528-529.

— « Note sur la gnose ou l'enseignement religieux des savants et des simples selon S. Thomas », *Bulletin Thomiste,* VIII (1931), Notes et Comm. 5*-7*.

— « S. Thomas, serviteur de la vérité », *Vie Spirituelle,* (mars, 1937), pp. 259-279.

— « Théologie », *Dictionnaire de théologie Catholique,* XVI¹, cc. 341-502.

DEFERRARI, R. J., PH. D., SISTER M. INVIOLATA BARRY, C. D. P., IGNATIUS MC GUINESS, O.P., *A Lexicon of St. Thomas Aquinas based on the Summa Theologica and selected passages of his other works.* Washington, D. C. : The Catholic University of America Press. Fascicles I-IV (A-Q). Five Fascicles to appear. 1948 —.

DRAGUET, R., « Méthodes théologiques d'hier et d'aujord'hui », *La Revue catholique des Idées et des Faits,* 10 janvier 1936, pp. 1-7; 7 février, pp. 4-7; 14 février, pp. 13-17.

DURKHEIM, EMILE, *L'évolution pédagogique en France,* 2 vol. — Vol. I : *Des origines à la Renaissance.* Paris : Lib. Felix Alcan, 1938.

ESTEBAN, A. AVELINO, « Nota bibliográfica sobre la llamada ' Teologia Nueva ' », *Revista Española de Teologia,* IX (1949), pp. 303-318.

FENTON, J. C., *The Concept of Sacred Theology.* Milwaukee : Bruce, 1941, pp. IX-276.

FRIEDERICHS, J., *Die Theologie als spekulative und praktische Wissenschaft nach Bonaventura und Thomas von Aquin.* Bonn, 1940.

GAGNEBET, R., O.P., « La nature de la théologie speculative », *Revue Thomiste,* XLIV (1938), pp. 1-39, 213-255, 645-674.

— « Un essai sur le problème théologique », *Revue Thomiste.* XLV (1939), pp. 108-145.

GARDEIL, A., O.P., *La donné révélé et la théologie.* Pref. par M.-D. Chenu, O.P., Juvisy : Ed. du Cerf, 1932, pp. XXXVI-372.

GARDET, L. and M. M. ANAWATI, *Introduction à la théologie Musulmane. Essai de théologie comparée.* (Etudes de philosophie médiévale XXXVII). Paris : J. Vrin, 1948, pp. VII-543.

124

GARRIGOU-LAGRANGE, R., O.P., « Actus specificatur ab obiecto formali », *Acta Pont. Academiae Romanae S. T. Aq.*, *1934*. Romae: Marietti, 1935, pp. 139-153.

— *De Deo Uno. Commentarium in Primam Partem S. Thomae.* Paris: Desclée de Brouwer, 1938, pp. 582.

— « De methodo S. Thomae, speciatim de structura articulorum Summae Theologicae », *Angelicum*, V *(*1928*)*, pp. 499-524.

— *Theologia Fundamentalis secundum S. Thomae Doctrinam. Pars Apologetica. De Revelatione per Ecclesiam Catholicam Proposita.* Romae: F. Ferrari, 1945, 2 vol.

GHELLINCK, J. DE, « Pour l'histoire du mot *revelare* », *Recherches de Science Religieuse*, VI (1916), pp. 149-157.

GILLET, M. S., O.P., *Lettre Encyclique sur l'enseignement de Saint Thomas à l'heure présente.* Romae: Typ. Pol. Vatic., 1943, pp. 102.

GILSON ETIENNE, *Reason and Revelation in the Middle Ages.* New-York: Scribner's, 1938, pp. 114.

— *L'être et l'essence.* Paris: J. Vrin, 1948, pp. 329.

— *Le Thomisme.*[5] Paris: J. Vrin, 1947, pp. 552.

GLORIEUX, P., *La littérature quodlibétique*: Vol. I: *La littérature quodlibétique de 1260 à 1320.* (Bibl. Thom. V). Kain (Belgique): Le Saulchoir, 1925, pp. 382. Vol. II: *La littérature quodlibétique.* (Bibl. Thom. XXI). Paris: J. Vrin, 1935, pp. 387.

— « Les 572 Questions du manuscrit de Douai 434 », *Recherches de Théologie Ancienne et Médiévale*, X (1938), pp. 123-152, 225-267.

— *Répertoire des maîtres en théologie de Paris au XIII*e *siècle.* (Etudes de Philosophie Médiévale XVII-XVIII), Paris: J. Vrin, 1933, 2 vol.

GRABMANN, M., « Commentatio historica in prologum Summa theologiae S. Thomae Aq. », *Angelicum*, III (1926), pp. 146-165.

— « Il concetto di scienza secondo S. Tommaso d'Aquino e le relazioni della fede e della teologia con la filosofia e le scienze profane », *Rivista di Filosofia Neo-Scolastica*, XXVI (1934), pp. 127-155.

— « De questione ' Utrum theologia sit scientia speculativa an practica ' a B. Alberto Magno et S. Thoma Aquinate pertractata », *Atti della Settimana Albertina.* Romae, 1932, pp. 107-126.

— « De theologia ut scientia argumentativa secundum S. Albertum Magnum et S. Thomam Aquinatem », *Angelicum*, XIV (1937), pp. 39-60.

— *Die theologische Erkenntnis- und Einleitungslehre des heiligen Thomas von Aquin, auf Grund seiner Schrift « In Boethium de Trinitate ».* Im Zusammenhang der Scholastick des 13. und beginnenden 14. Jahrhunderts dargestellt. (Thomistische Studien, IV. Band.) Freiburg in der Schweiz, Paulusverlag, 1948, pp. XV-392.

— *Die Werke des hl. Thomas von Aquin.*[3] (Beiträge zur Geschichte der Philosophie und Theologie des Mittelalters, Band XXII. Heft 1-2). Münster i. W., Aschendorff, 1949, pp. XIX-479.

GUIBERT, J. DE, S.J., *Les doublets de S. Thomas. Leur étude méthodique. Quelques réflexions, quelques exemples.* Paris: Beauchesne, 1926, pp. 164.

GUZZETTI, G. B., « Saggio bibliographico sulla ' theologia della predicazione ' »,
La Scuola Cattolica LXXVII (1950), pp. 350-356. (Fascicle IV-V (1950) of
La Scuola Cattolica is devoted entirely to the subject of *Verkündigungstheo-logie*).

GUZZO, A., *Tommaso d'Aquino. Il Maestro*. Trad., Introd., Commento. Firenze:
Vallecchi, 1928, pp. 65.

JOANNES A SANCTO THOMA, O.P., *Cursus Theologicus*. Opere et studio monacho-rum quorumdam Solesmensium, O.S.B., editus. Paris-Roma-Tournai: Desclée,
1931-1937. 3 vol.

JOURNET, CHARLES, *Introduction à la théologie*. Paris: Desclée de Brouwer, 1947,
pp. 331.

KILWARDBY, ROBERT, O.P., *In Sententias P. Lombardi* (Oxford, Merton College
Mss. 131). Prologue edited by F. Stegmüller, Roberti Kilwardby *De Natura
Theologiae*, Münster, 1935.

KLUBERTANZ, G. P., S.J., « The Unity of Human Activity », *The Modern School-man, XXVII* (1950), pp. 75-103.

LABOURDETTE, M., O.P., « La théologie, intelligence de la foi », *Revue Thomiste*,
LII (1946), pp. 26-34.

LABOURDETTE, M.-NICOLAS, R.-L. BRUCKBERGER, O.P., *Dialogue théologique.
Pièces du débat entre « La Revue Thomiste » d'une part et les R.R. P.P. de
Lubac, Daniélou, Bouillard, Fessard, von Balthasar, S. J., d'autre part.*
Saint Maximin, Var: Les Arcades, 1947, pp. 151.

LANG, A., « Die Gliederung und die Reichweite des Glaubens nach Thomas von
Aquin und den Thomisten », *Divus Thomas* (Fribourg), XX (1942), pp. 228-235.

LONERGAN, B., S.J., « St. Thomas' Theory of Operation », *Theological Studies*,
III (1942), pp. 374-402.

LOTTIN, O., O.S.B., « Quelques ' Quaestiones ' de maîtres parisiens aux environs
de 1225-1235 », *Recherches de Théologie Ancienne et Médiévale*, V (1933),
pp. 79-95.

MANDONNET, PIERRE, O.P., *Des écrits authentiques de S. Thomas d'Aquin*. (Se-conde édition revue et corrigée). Fribourg (Suisse): Imprimerie de l'Oeuvre
de saint-Paul, 1910, pp. 158.
Cf. Reviews:
> *Bulletin de Littérature ecclésiastique*, IV (1912), pp. 175-180. (by Remi
> Hourcade).
> *Zeitschrift für katholische Theologie*, 41 (1917), pp. 820-832. (by F.
> Pelster).

MANDONNET, P., O.P., ET J. DESTREZ, O.P., *Bibliographie Thomiste*. (Bibliothèque
Thomiste I). Kain (Belgique): Le Saulchoir, 1921, pp. XXI-116.

MANDONNET, P., O.P., (ed.). *S. Thomae Scriptum super Libros Sententiarum Ma-gistri Petri Lombardi*, editio nova. Paris: Lethielleux, 1929-1947, 4 vol. (M.
F. Moos, O. P., became editor with vol. III).

MARIN-SOLA, F., O.P., *L'Evolution homogène du Dogme Catholique.*² Paris: V.
Lecoffre, 1924. 2 vol.

126

MARITAIN, J., *Distinguer pour unir ou les degrés du savoir*. Paris: Desclée de Brouwer, 1932, pp. XVII-919.

— *Science et sagesse*. Paris: Labergerie, 1915, pp. 393.

MARROU, H. I., « ‘Doctrina’ et ‘Disciplina’ dans la langue des Pères de l’Eglise », *Bulletin du Cange: Archivum Latinitatis Medii Aevi*, IX (1934), pp. 5-25.

MARTIN, R. M., O.P., « L’objet integral de la théologie d’après saint Thomas et les Scholastiques », *Revue Thomiste*, XX (1912), pp. 12-21.

MAYER, M. H., *The Philosophy of Teaching of St. Thomas*. Introd. by E. A. Fitzpatrick. Milwaukee: Bruce, 1929, pp. 164.

MERSCH, E., S.J., « Le Christ mystique centre de la théologie comme science », *Nouvelle Revue Théologique*, LXI (1934), pp. 449-475.

— « L’objet de la théologie et le ‘Christus totus’ », *Recherches de Science Religieuse*, XXVI (1936), pp. 129-157.

MICHELITSCH, ANTON, *Thomasschriften 1*. (Philosophische Reihe. Band I: *Bibliographisches*). Graz und Wien: Styria, 1913, pp. XII-252.

— *Thomasschriften 2*. (Theologische Reihe. Band I: *Kommentatoren zur Summa Theologie des hl. Thomas von Aquin*). Graz und Wien: Styria, 1924, pp. 203.

MORANDO, D., « Sul ‘De magistro’ di S. Tommaso », *Rivista Rosminiana di Filosofia e di Cultura*, XXV, 1931.

RABEAU, GASTON, *Introduction à l’étude de la théologie*. Paris: Bloud et Gay, 1926, pp. XII-413.

RICHARD, TH., *Comment étudier et situer saint Thomas*. Paris: Lethielleux, 1938, pp. 228.

RIMAUD, J., S. J., *Thomisme et Méthode*. Paris: Beauchesne, 1925, pp. 224.

RIVIÈRE, J., « Theologia », *Revue des Sciences Religieuses*, XVI (1936), pp. 47-57.

ROSCHINI, GABRIELE M., O.S.M., *Introductio in S. Theologiam*. Romae: Officium Libri Catholici, 1947, pp. 112.

— « La Theologia è Veramente Scienza? » *Acta Pont. Academiae Romanae S. Thomas Aq. et Religionis Catholicae*, X (1945), pp. 47-132.

RUNG, R., « Studio sulla ‘Quaestio disp. De Magistro’ S. Tommaso d’Aquino », *Rivista di Filosofia Neoscolastica*, XIV (1922), pp. 109-165.

SCHÜTZ, LUDWIG, *Thomaslexikon, Sammlung, Übersetzung, und Erklärung der in sämtlichen Werken des hl. Thomas v. Aquin vorkommenden Kunstausdrücke und wissenschaftlichen Aussprüche.*[2] Paderborn: Ferdinand Schöningh, 1895.

SERTILLANGES, A. D., O.P., *Saint Thomas d’Aquin. Somme Théologique. Dieu*. Tome I. Traduction française. Paris-Tournai-Rome, Desclée et Cie., 1925, pp. 372.

SOLANO, JESUS, S.J., *El Problema Teologico*. Madrid: Aldecoa, 1943.

SPIAZZI, R., O.P. (ed.), *S. Thomae Aq. Quaestiones Quodlibetales*. Editio VIII revisa. Taurini-Romae: Marietti, 1949, pp. 269.

— *S. Thomae Aq. Quaestiones Disputatae*. Editio VIII revisa. Taurini-Romae: Marietti, 1949, 2 vol.

STEGMÜLLER, F., *Repertorium Commentariorum Sententias Petri Lombardi*. Herbipoli (Würzburg): F. Schöningh, 1947, 2 vol.

STOLZ, A., O.S.B, *Introductio in Sacram Theologiam.* Friburgi Brisgoviae: Herder, 1941, pp. 134.

SYLVIUS, FRANCISCUS, Opera Omnia. Tomi VI. — Tomi I: *Commentarii in Totam Primam Partem S. Thomae Aquinatis Doctoris Angelici et Communis.* Antuerpiae, 1714.

THOMAS AQUINAS, S., O.P., *Opera Omnia jussu impensaque Leonis XIII, P. M., edita.* Romae: R. Garroni, 1882 — (incomplete: 15 volumes have appeared to date).

— *Opera Omnia.* Parma, 1852-1873, 25 vol.

— *Summa contra Gentiles.* (Editio leonina manualis). Romae: apud Sedem Commissionis Leoninae, et apud Librariam Vaticanam; Desclée-Herder, 1934, pp. VI-581.

— *Summa Theologiae* cura et studio Instituti Studiorum Medievalium Ottaviensis ad textum S. Pii Pp. V jussu confectum recognita. Ottawa (Canada): Studium Generale O.P., 1941-1945, 5 vol.

TONNEAU, JEAN, O.P., [Comptes Rendus: J. M. Ramirez, O.P., *De hominis beatitudine ...*], *Bulletin Thomiste,* VII (1943-1946), pp. 7-45.

WYSER, PAUL, O.P., *Theologie als Wissenschaft. Ein Beitrag zur theologischen Erkenntnislehre.* Salzburg-Leipzig: A. Pustet, 1938, pp. 218.

— *Thomas von Aquin. In Librum Boethii de Trinitate Quaestiones Quinta et Sexta nach dem Autograph Cod. Vat. lat. 9850 mit Einleitung ...* Fribourg: Societé Philosophique; Louvain: Edition E. Nauwelaerts, 1948, pp. 80.

ZAPELENA, T., S. J., « Problema theologicum », *Gregorianum,* XXIV (1943), pp. 23-47, 287-326; XXV (1944), pp. 38-73, 247-282.

INDEX

ACTION: in the patient, 70; reception of, depends on recipient, 81; *sacra doctrina* as, 49 f., 79-82, 84, 89, 96, 104, 110 ff., 116 f.

AMANN, Msgr., 15

ANALOGY: between habit and operation of science, 99 f., 110, 107 f.; between meanings of *doctrina*, 74 f.; between meanings of *sacra doctrina*, 95 f.; between *sacra doctrina* and habit of theology, 99 ff., 110; used in *sacra doctrina*, 111 f.

ANGELS: teaching of, 54

ARISTOTLE, 30, 81, 91; on acquisition of science, 56 f.; use of term *doctrina* in, 51 f.

ART: imitates nature, 58 f.

AUGUSTINE, 53, 56, 89

AUTHORITY OF TEACHER, 63

AVERROES: on unity of possible intellect, 66

AVICENNA, 56

BACON, R., 12

BARTHELEMY DE BOLOGNE, 14

BILLUART, C. R., O.P.: on meaning of *sacra doctrina*, 26, 34 note, 50

BONAVENTURE, ST., 12 note

BONNEFOY, J.-Fr., O.F.M.
comment on *in I Sent.*, prol., q. 1, a. 1, 45
comment on *S. T.*, I, q. 1, a. 1, ad 1, 39-44
comment on *S. T.*, I, q. 1 a. 2, ad 2, 96
defective interpretation by, 44, 47

BONNEFOY (continued)
on equivalence of *sacra doctrina* and *theologia*, 36, 38
on meaning of *sacra doctrina*, 35-47, 50
procedure of, in investigating *sacra doctrina*, 35-39, 88, f.
on relation of *sacra doctrina* with Scripture, 35-38, 96, 98
on *revelabile* in St. Thomas, 36, 44
on *sacra doctrina* as *scientia*, 88

BOYER, C., S. J., 9

BULLETIN THOMISTE, 49

CAJETAN, TOMAS DE VIO CARD., O.P.: 13, 88 f., 91; comments on *S. T.*, I, q. 1, a. 1, 18 ff.; comments on *S. T.*, I, q. 1, a. 2, 21; comments on *S. T.*, I, q. 1, a. 3, 22; on meaning of *sacra doctrina*, 17 ff., 22 f., 50

CAUSALITY: of teaching (*doctrina*), 64; of *sacra doctrina*, 49 f., 77, 116 f.

CAUSE
of diversity of *doctrina*, 72 f.
of opinion, 59
per se of knowledge, 71, f.
principal and instrumental, 58
of science, 59 f.
of unity of *doctrina*, 72 f.
of unity of science, 98 f., 106 ff.

CERTITUDE: cause of, 63

CHENU, M.-D., O.P., 11, 68 note, 83 note, 93 note, 95 note; on ambiguity of term *sacra doctrina*, 31 f., 103; on meaning of *sacra doctrina*, 31 ff., 50; on unity of first question of *Summa*, 33, 111

129

9

COMMUNICATION OF GOD'S GIFTS: hierarchical character of, 12, 79 f., 118
CONCLUSIONS: certitude of, 63; theological, and theology, 83, 114 f.
CONGAR, Yves M.-J., O.P.: on Bonnefoy's interpretation, 47; on *sacra doctrina* in St. Thomas, 11 ff., 47-50; on *sacra doctrina* as *scientia*, 48 f.; on the term *revelabile*, 15; on univocity of term *sacra doctrina*, 49
CONSISTERE IN: various senses of, 41 f.
CONTEMPLATIVE LIFE: as principle of teaching, 65
CONTEMPLATION: twofold, 46
COOPERATION WITH GOD: in governing world, 13

DARQUENNES, A., S. J., 14 note
DEFERRARI, R. J., 52 note
DEMONSTRATION: cause of science, 59, 68 f., 71 f.
DENZINGER, 12
DICTIONNAIRE DE THEOLOGIE CATHOLIQUE, 14, 49
DIONYSIUS, 12, 54
DISCIPLE: activity of, in learning, 59 ff., 68; begins by believing, 31 f; intellectual dispositions of, 62, 68; teaching adapted to capacity of, 55, 68, 76 f., 119
DISCIPLINA: notion of, 51, 58, 69 f., 87; order of, 68 and note, 95, 112
DISCOVERY, 58 f., 67
DIVERSITY: in *doctrina*, 72; of science, 106 f.
DOCTIO: used for *doctrina*, 69
DOCTRINA (in St. Thomas)
in active sense, 11 and note, 51 f., 64 f., 67 f., 70, 73 f.
an analogous term, 70 f., 74
as artificial action, 67 f.
Congar on meaning of, 11 f.
defined in terms of its causes, 64
distinct from *scientia*, 93 f.
essentials of notion of, 63, 71
formal sense of term, 64-69, 74, 77, 87
generic signification of, 72 f., 75
imitates discovery, 59, 67
John of St. Thomas on meaning of, 29 f.

DOCTRINA (continued)
per modum locutionis, 66, 79, 118
objective meaning of, 73 f.
as participation in government of world, 13
predicated of *scientia*, 75
proprie et improprie dicta, 71
reasoning process in, 54-63, 67 f., 71 f.
relation to verbal discourse of teacher, 55, 60, 65-68, 74
relation of written word to, 97
scientia in active sense of, 75, 91-94
theology as, 27 f., 45 f.
Thomas on Aristotle's use of term, 51 f.
unity of, 72 f.
various senses of term, 12, 64 f., 73 f., 94; *see also* THEACHING, *Sacra Doctrina*
DOGMA: development of, 15

ENDS OF SACRA DOCTRINA, 13 f., 49, 83 f., 114, 118
EUDES RIGAUD, 12 note

FAITH
Cajetan on 'explicitation' of, 21 f.
distinguished from habit of theology, 32
relation of, to *sacra doctrina*, 32, 46 f., 81, 87, 117
sacra doctrina and truths accepted on, 39-44, 46 f.
sacra doctrina terminates first in, 81 f., 90, 111
Sylvius on necessity of, 26
teaching of knowledge accepted on, 59, 72
universal principles as cause of, 59
FORM: eduction of, 56; pre-existence of, in matter, 57 f.
FORMAL OBJECT: and formal subject of science, 106 f.; of potency or habit, 98, 101, 105; of sacred theology, 98-101, 109; of a science, 98 f.; and unity of science, 106 ff.
FORMAL SUBJECT: and formal object of science, 106 f.; of natural theology, 109 f.; of *sacra doctrina*, 108 f.; of a science, 105-108

GAGNEBET, M.-R., O.P., 33, 50 f.
GARRIGOU-LAGRANGE, R., O.P., 33 f., 50
GENUS : *doctrina* signifies as, 72 f.
GHELLINCK, J. DE, 15 note
GILBERT DE LA PORREE, 12 note
GILSON, ETIENNE, 9, 15, 79 note; on
    meaning of *revelabile*, 109
GLORIEUX, P., 53 note
GOD : principal cause of *sacra doctrina*,
    49 f., 59, 116; procession of creatures
    from, and return to, 14; teaches inte-
    riorly, 56, 59, 67; subject of *sacra
    doctrina*, 108 ff.
GRABMANN, M., 33
GUELLUY, R., 13 note
GUIBERT, J. De, 15 note

HABIT : acquired in *sacra doctrina*,
    93 f.; formal object of 98 f., 105; of
    sacred theology and *sacra doctrina*,
    94 f. 116
HILARY, ST., 13 note
HISTORY : twofold process in, 14
HORACE, 52 note

INCORPORATION IN CHRIST : twofold, 13
IMPRESSIO SCIENTIAE DIVINAE, 101 f.
INTELLECT : Averroes on unity of possi-
    ble, 66; collocative power of, 61 f.,
    68; dispositions of, 62, 68; first
    conceptions of, 57 f.; function of
    agent, 60; light of, 54
INTELLIGIBLE OBJECT : as presented by
    teacher, 54 f., 61 f.
INTELLIGIBLE SPECIES : words signs
    of, 60
INSTRUCTION ; *see* teaching, *doctrina*,
    sacra doctrina; economy of Christian,
    12 ff.; by way of revelation, 79-84,
    118
INVENTIO, 58 f., 67
INVIOLATA BARRY, SISTER M., 52 note

JOHN OF ST. GILES, 12 note
JOHN OF ST. THOMAS, O.P.: on the
    term, *doctrina*, 29 f.; on meaning of
    sacra doctrina, 27-31, 50; on ne-
    cessity of theology, 31; on unity of
    theology, 27

KILWARDBY, R., 95
KNOWLEDGE ; see also *scientia*
    characteristics of scientific, 94
    goal of perfect, 83
    imparted by *sacra doctrina*, 87
    modes of, 42 f.; see *scientia*
    reduction from potential to actual,
    59 f.
    teacher *per se* cause of, 71 f.
KLUBERTANZ, G., S. J., 9, 114

LATERAN COUNCIL 1215, 12
LEARNING ; *see disciplina*
LECLERCQ, J., 13 note
LOCUS CLASSICUS : on nature of *do-
    ctrina*, 52
    on nature of theology, 7
LANDGRAF, A., 12
LOMBARD PETER, 31
LONERGAN, B., S. J., 70
LOTTIN, O., 53 note

MAGISTERIUM OF THE CHURCH : and
    revelation, 79 f., and *sacra doctrina*,
    114, 117
MAN : as teacher, 52, 54 f.
MARROU, H. I., 12 note
MC GUINESS, I. O.P., 52 note
METAPHOR: in *sacra doctrina*, 7 f.,111 ff.
METHOD : in teaching, 68; in Scripture
    and *sacra doctrina*, 111 f.; *see also*
    order
MICHELITSCH, A., 17
MIDDLE AGES ; ideal of unity in 14,
    114
MOTTE, A., O.P., 13 note.
MOVEMENT (motus): in action and
    passion identical, 70; of reason in
    doctrina, 59 f., 70, 72 f.
MÜCKSHOFF, M., 15 note

NATURE : operation of, in teaching, 59;
    of *sacra doctrina*, 8, 114

OPERATION : nature of, in teaching, 59;
    revelation, a hierarchical, 79 f., 118;
    unity of *sacra doctrina* as an, 114
OPINION : causes of, 59; in theological
    science, John of St. Thomas on, 27

ORDER: of learning (*ordo disciplinae*), 68 and note, 95, 112; in Scripture and *sacra doctrina*, 38, 112

PARTICIPATION: forms of, in government of world, 13
PASSIO: identical in movement with *actio*, 70
PECKHAM, 12 note
PELSTER, F., S. J., 9
PLATONISTS, 56
POTENCY: active and passive, 57; accidental and essential, 61
PRINCIPLES: cause of faith and opinion, 59; for interpreting meaning of *sacra doctrina*, 21, 35 f., 39, 88; of knowledge, function of, 51 f., 54, 61 ff., 70 f.; of *sacra doctrina*, 42, 83 ff.; of unity and diversity in science, 42 f., 106 ff.
PROPHECY: St. Thomas on, 101

REASON: process in *doctrina*, 59 f., 70 ff.; light of, 59; science, a process of, 106 ff.; unity of movement of, 72 f.; process in discovery, 59
REVEALED TRUTH: *sacra doctrina* 'consists in', 39-44, 85; see also *truth*.
REVELABILE (in St. Thomas): Bonnefoy on, 36, 44; Congar on, 15; Gilson on, 15, 109; formal object of sacred theology, 108 f.
REVELATUM: *formaliter et virtualiter*, Bonnefoy on, in St. Thomas, 45
REVELATION: instruction by way of, 79-84, 118; participated forms of, 80, 117 f.; relation of, to *sacra doctrina*, 15 f., 79 f., 98, 117 f.; Thomas' notion of 15, 79, f., 118
ROBERT OF MELUM, 12 note
RIMAUD, J., S. J., 35
ROLAND OF CREMONA, O.P., 12 note
SACRA DOCTRINA (in St. Thomas)
in the *Commentary*, 84 f
in prologue of *Summa*, 76 f.
in first article of *Summa*, 77-88
in second article, 88-98
in third article, 98-103
in fourth article, 103
in fifth article, 104

SACRA DOCTRINA (in St. Thomas)
in sixth article, 104
in seventh article, 105-110
in eighth article, 110
in ninth and tenth articles, 110-114
accommodated to condition of nature, 81 f.
action of a teacher, 49 f., 79-82, 84, 89, 96, 104, 110 ff., 116 f.
analogous senses of term, 95 f.
author's interpretation of, 49 f., 89, 110, 116 f.
Billuart's interpretation of, 26, 34 note, 50
Bonnefoy's interpretation of, 35-47, 50
Bonnefoy on relation of Scripture to, 35-38, 96, 98
Cajetan's interpretation of, 17-23, 50
Cajetan on generic signification of, 18, 20 f.
Chenu on ambiguity of term, 31 f., 103
Chenu on meaning of, 31 ff., 50
Congar on, 11 ff., 47-50
« consists in » revealed truth, 39-44, 85
causality of, 49 f, 77, 116 f.
development in use of term, 84, 119
distinguished from Scripture, 37
eschatological character of, 14
finality of, 13 f., 49, 83 f., 114, 118
Gagnebet's interpretation of, 33, 50
Garrigou-Lagrange's interpretation of, 33 ff., 50
gives birth to faith, 19 f., 89 f.
habit acquired in, 93 f.
importance of meaning of, 7 f.
impressio scientiae divinae, 100 ff.
instrumental causality in, 49 f., 116 f.
John of St. Thomas' interpretation of, 27-31
meaning of, in Lombard's time, 31
per modum revelationis, 79 f., 118
necessary for salvation, 30 f., 42, 79, 84
is one science, 98-103
operation of God in, 116, f.
opposed to philosophical disciplines, 36
origin, principle, term of, 85

SACRA DOTTRINA (in S. Thomas)
participation of revelation, 118
principal cause of, 49 f., 59, 116
principles for interpreting meaning
of, 21, 35 f., 39, 88 f.
proceeds under light of faith, 80
progress in, 82-85
as related to development of dogma, 15
relation of, to habit of sacred theology, 86 f., 93, 99 f.
relation of, to Scripture, 22, 49, 77,
96 ff., 112, 116
relation of, to habit of sacred theology, 49, 94 f.
and revelation, 15 f., 79 f , 98, 117 f.
Rimaud's interpretation of, 35
has same sense throughout first question, 17 ff., 47 f., 95, 110
as *scientia*, 86-96, 105-108
scientific character of, 85 f.
and Scriptural exegesis, 113 f.
Sertillanges' interpretation of, 26 f., 50
stages of, 82-85
supernatural wisdom as end of, 49,
83 f., 118
Sylvius' interpretation of, 23-26, 50
terminates first in faith, 81 f., 90,
111 f.
texts on ; *see* Thomas Aquinas
Thomas' preference for term, 53, 87,
119
and truths accepted on faith, 39-44
unity of, 98-103
various interpretations of, 50
SACRED SCRIPTURE
basic text of *sacra doctrina*, 112, 114
Bonnefoy on relation of *sacra doctrina*
to, 35-38, 96, 98
exegesis of, in *sacra doctrina*, 113 f.
infallible guide in *sacra doctrina*,
97 f., 112
ordered to Christian wisdom, 49, 97,
116
relation of, to *sacra doctrina*, 49, 96
ff. 110-113, 116
use of metaphor in, 111 f.
SCHÜTZ, L., 52 and note
SCIENTIA
in active sense of *doctrina*, 75, 91-94
an analogous concept, 75

SCIENTIA (continued)
Bonnefoy on *sacra doctrina* as, 38
Cajetan on *sacra doctrina* as, 21 f.
cause of diversity in, 42 f., 86 f., 106
caused by words of teacher, 60
Congar on *sacra doctrina* as, 48 and
note
distinction between *doctrina* and
habit of, 93 f.
doctrina as predicated of, 74 f.
formal object of, 98, 101, 105-108
formal subject of, 105-108
impression of divine, 97, 101 f.
John of St Thomas on theology as,
27 f.
method of acquiring, 56-62, 67 f.
method of teaching, 59 f., 67 f., 72
notion of, 70 f , 106 f.
as an operation of reason, 89-92,
106 ff.
pre-exists potentially in disciple, 58 f.,
61 ff., 65 f
principle of unity in, 98 ff., 106 ff.
proprie et improprie dicta, 71
propter quid and *quia*, 62, 69, 71 f.
proximate cause of, 60
sacra doctrina as, 86-96, 105-108
subalternation of, 93 note
Thomas' use of term, 21 f., 62, 90-94
unity of, 98 ff , 106 ff.
SERTILLANGES, 26 f., 50
STEGMULLER, F., 53 note
STEPHEN OF TOURNAI, 12 n te
SUBALTERNATION : of science, 90, 93
note
SUBJECT ; see formal subject
SYLVIUS, F. : on meaning of
sacra doctrina, 23-27, 50 ; on necessity of theology for salvation, 25 f.

TEACHER
beginning to teach, 82 f., 119
and capacity of disciples, 55, 68, 76
f , 82, 119
the Christian, 13, 14 note, 76 f., 119
function of a, 59-68, 71 f.
function of words of, 60
God as man's, 18, 49, 47 note, 59,
80 f., 111, 116
notion of, 54 f., 59 ff.

133

TEACHER (continued)
per se cause of knowledge, 62, 71 f.
of sacred theology, 119
and *sacra doctrina*, 49 f., 56, 76 f.,
  81 ff., 116 f.
St Thomas as model, 119
verbal discourse of, 55, 60, 64 f., 74

TEACHING; *see also doctrina*, teacher
analogous with curing, 59
by angels, 54
an artificial action, 67 f.
begins from previous knowledge, 51
  f., 63
causality involved in, 64 ff.
and contemplative life, 65
certitude in, 63
defined by its causes, 64
essentials of notion of, 63, 71
of first principles, 71 f.
formal element of, 64 f., 68, 74
function of words in, 55, 60, 65-68, 74
grace not required in, 56
internally by God, 56, 59, 67
of knowledges not scientific, 56, 63, 72
by man, 54 ff., 59, 67
«picture method» of, in Scripture, 111
principal agent in, 57 note, 59
procedure in, 66 ff., 74, 119
reasoning process in, 54-63, 67 f., 71 f.
Thomas' notion of, 59 f., 63 ff., 67, 71
of truths received on faith, 40 ff.,
  62 f., 81 f.
ways of teaching, 54 f., 62, 74

THEOLOGIA: Bonnefoy on medieval
usage of term, 36 f.; Bonnefoy on
notion of, in St. Thomas, 36 f., 38,
45; Cajetan's use of term, 20;
Congar on Thomas' use of term,
12 note; *quae Sacra Scriptura
dicitur*, 37 and note, 109; Sylvius'
meaning of, 23

THEOLOGICAL CONCLUSIONS: and theology, 83, 114 f.

THEOLOGY, SACRED
and Catholic education, 118
the Christian Wisdom, 114 f., 118 f.
generically different from natural
theology, 86 f., 108 f.
John of St. Thomas on necessity of,
28, 30 f.

THEOLOGY, SACRED (continued)
for the layman, 14 note, 118
relation of *sacra doctrina* to habit
  of, 49, 86, 99-103
relation of Scripture to habit of, 49,
  97 f., 116
Sylvius on necessity of, 25 f.

THOMAS AQUINAS, ST.
Billuart on *sacra doctrina* in, 26, 34
  note, 50
Cajetan on *sacra doctrina* in, 17 ff., 50
Chenu on *sacra doctrina* in, 31 ff., 50
Congar on *sacra doctrina* in, 11 ff.,
  47-50
development in concept of *sacra
  doctrina* in, 84, 119
Gagnebet on *sacra doctrina* in, 33, 50
Garrigou-Lagrange on *sacra doctrina*
  in, 33 f., 50
Grabmann on *sacra doctrina* in, 33
John of St. Thomas on *sacra doctrina*
  in, 27-31, 50
meaning of *doctrina* in, 51-75; *see
  doctrina*
meaning of *sacra doctrina* in, 76-117;
  see sacra doctrina
notion of revelation in, 79 f., 118
preference for term *sacra doctrina*,
  53, 87, 119
on purpose of *Summa Theologica*,
  76 f.
Sertillanges on *sacra doctrina* in, 26
  f., 50
Sylvius on *sacra doctrina* in, 23-27, 50
TEXTS CITED FROM
in I Sent., prol., q. 1, a. 1 (45); a. 1,
  sol. (46, 94); a. 1, ad 1 (84); a. 3,
  sol. 1 (83, 94); a. 3, sol. 2 (93);
  a. 3, sol. 3 (83); a. 3, qa. 2, ad
  aliud (93)
in II Sent., d. 9, q. 1, a. 2, ad 4 (53,
  66, 73); d. 28, q. 1, a. 5, ad 3
  (55)
*Contra impugnantes Dei cultum et
  religionem*, c. 2 (12)
Quest. disp. de Veritate., q. 11 (52);
  a. 1c (56-59, 64, 73); obj. 3, 6, 12
  (64); ad 3 (65); ad 4 (60, 65); ad
  6 (64); ad 11 (60); ad 12 (60, 64);
  ad 13 (63); ad 16 (64); a. 4, ad 1,

THOMAS AQUINAS, ST.
TEXTS CITED FROM (continued)
(80); q. 14, a. 9, ad 3 (83); a. 10c
(81 f.)
Quest. Quodlibetales II, 6 (11); IV,
18 (119)
in Boethii de Trinitate, q. 5, a. 4c
(37, 109); a. 4, ad 8 (32 note); q. 6,
a. 1c (92); a. 4c (92)
Summa contra Gentiles I, 2 (13); II,
4 (11); II, 75 (53, 66 f.)
iu S. Pauli Apostoli epistolas, prol.
(12); in Rom., c. 1, lect. 5 (11);
in I Cor., c. 3. lect. 2 (12); in I
Cor., c. 12, lect. 3 (12 f.); in II
Tim., c. 4, lect. 1 (11); in Tit.,
c. 1, lect. 3 (12)
in X libros Ethicorum ad Nicoma-
chum, I, lect. 1 (11)
Summa Theologica, prol. (76 f.); I,
1, 1c (78); ad 1 (39, 85); ad 2
(85 ff.); a. 2, Sed Contra (89 f.);
ad 2 (96); a 3c (98 ff.); ad 1 (108);
ad 2 (100 f.); a. 4c (103); a. 5, ad
2 (104); a. 6c (104 f.); a 7c (105);
a 8 (110); a 9, 10 (110-114); q. 42,
a. 2c (70 note); q. 75, a. 5, obj. 1
(73); q. 117 (13); a. 1c (53, 68);
I-II, q. 19, a. 5 ad 1 (13); q. 34,
a. 1c (11); q. 57, a. 2, ad 1 (83);
II-II, q. 2, a. 3c (81); a 6c (12, 80);
q. 5, a. 3, ad 2 (12 f.); q. 171, a.
1c (101); a. 4, ad 2 (79); a. 6c
(101); q. 178, a. 2, ad 3 (73); q. 187,
a. 6, ad 3 (73); III, q. 7, a. 7 (11);
q. 35, a. 5 (12); q. 42 (11, 13);
a. 4c (97)
in VIII libros Physicorum, III, c. 2,
lect. 3 (69); c. 3, lect. 5 (64); V,
c. 2, lect. 3 (69)
in libros Post Anal., I, c. 1, lect. 1
(51); c. 1, lect. 3 (70); c. 28, lect.
41 (72, 91, 106 f.)

THOMAS AQUINAS, ST.
TEXT CITED FROM (continued)
in XII libros Metaphysicorum, VII,
lect. 17 (Cath. 1670-1) (69)
De Unitate Intellectus contra Aver-
roistas, c. 5 (53)
Quest. disp. de Caritate, a. 13 et ad
6 (12)
use of term, scientia, in, 21 f., 62,
90-94
TRUTHS: to be accepted on faith, 40,
42 ff., 83; as object of sacra doctrina
43 f., 99 f.; order of, in sacra doctrina, 38, 112; order of, in Scripture, 38, 112

UNITY
of Christian wisdom, 14, 114
in doctrina, cause of, 72 f.
of essence, of operation, 114
of first question of Summa, 18 ff.,
24, 33, 95, 111, 114, 116 ff.
Middle Ages' ideal of, 14, 114
of potency or habit, 98, 101
of sacra doctrina, 99 ff., 114 f.
of a science, 98 f., 106 ff.

VARIANT READINGS, 37 note, 40 f., 109
note
VIGNON, H., S. J., 9
VISION OF GOD: beatitude consists in,
41, 81; ultimate term of sacra doctrina, 83
VOLLERT, C., S. J., 9

WILLIAM OF MELITO, 12 note
WISDOM: as function of sacra doctrina,
104, 114 f., 118; right and duty to
pursue, 118 f.; sacra doctrina terminates in, 49 f., 83, 116 f.;
unity of Christian, 114 f.
WORDS: function of, in teaching, 60, 97